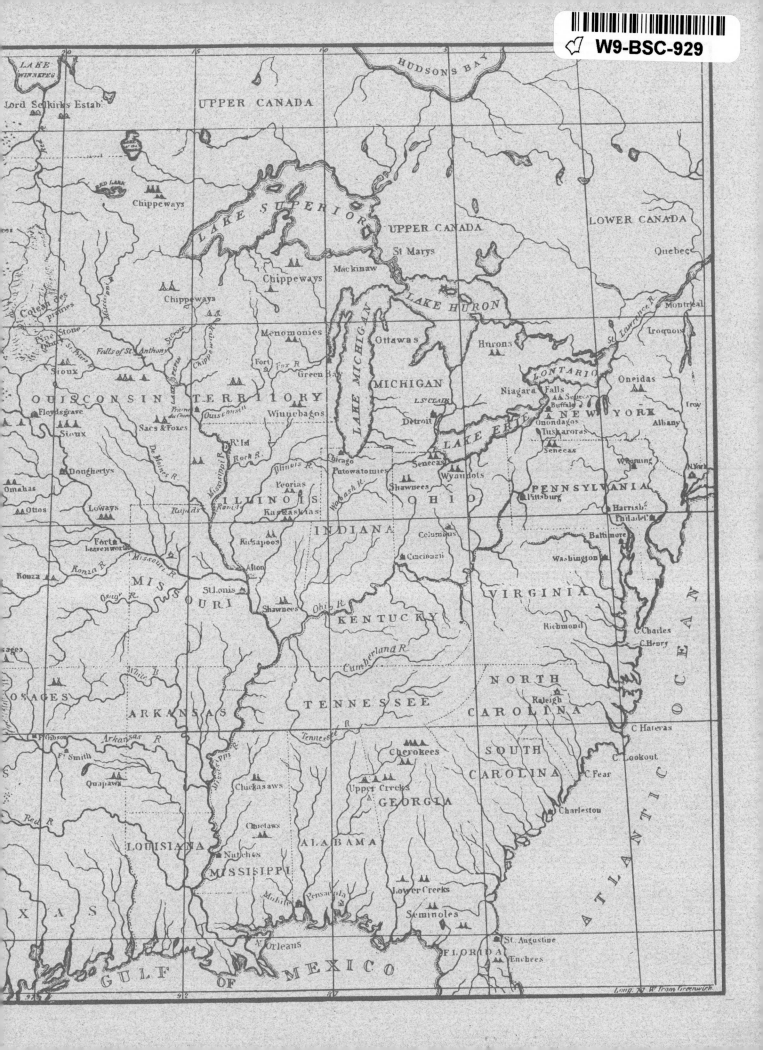

INDIAN BASKETS
OF
NORTH AMERICA

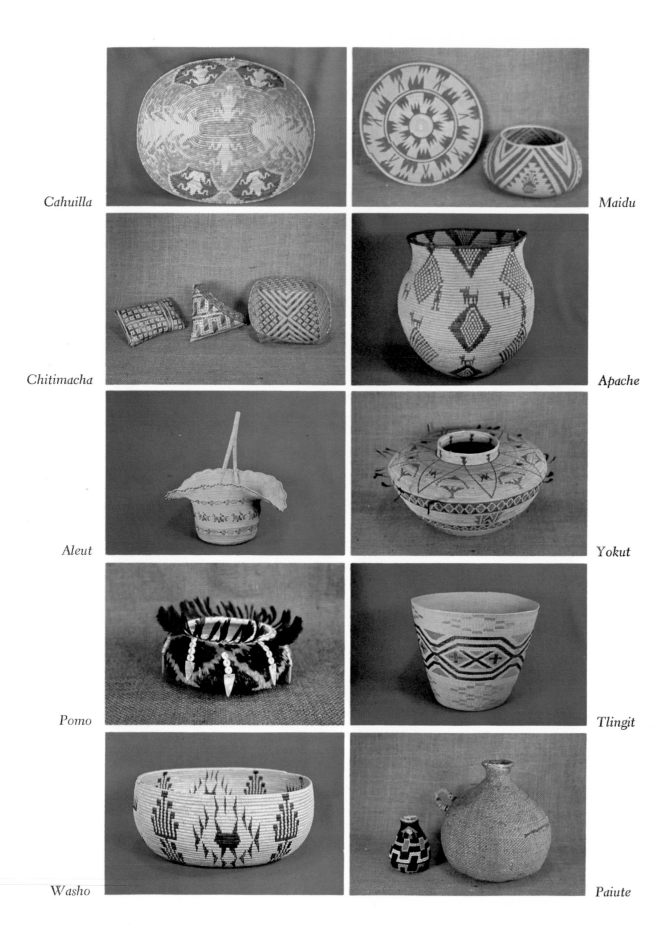

Cahuilla

Maidu

Chitimacha

Apache

Aleut

Yokut

Pomo

Tlingit

Washo

Paiute

INDIAN BASKETS OF NORTH AMERICA

Frank W. Lamb

by Dr. Frank W. Lamb

published by
Rubidoux Publishing Co.

Maps and Photographs

by

The Author

Jacket design by . . . . Ada Pidot
Drawings by . . . . . . Joy Cole

FOREWORD

Mankind has developed many kinds of art. We must not let ourselves believe that the art forms are restricted to civilized people. The early American Indians are proof to the contrary. The appreciation of these aboriginal people for color, form and design reaches far into the regions of the past, as is shown by their basketry.

Recent discoveries of basket fragments have been dated to more than 3,000 years before the time of Christ. Although most of the basket weaving was done by women, it was appreciated by all her peers. A woman who could design and weave well gained social status within her community.

It is intended that the following shall give some insight to the place of basketry in Indian culture. No book of this nature can possibly be complete nor can its content be beyond criticism. It is hoped that this book will help toward a better understanding and appreciation of North American Indian art.

F W L

Dedicated
to
The Women in my life

My Secretary

My Sweetheart

My Wife

Who Wear the Same Shoes

CONTENTS

INDIAN BASKETS OF NORTH AMERICA

Indian Baskets of North America

by

Dr. Frank W. Lamb

Introduction

This volume is intended to be a guide to anyone interested in collecting, identifying, or just reading about Indian basketry. I will follow a geographic pattern in this book's organization. It will begin in the extreme northwest at the Aleuts, following south and eastward down the coast of Alaska, British Columbia, Washington, Oregon, California, Nevada, Utah, Arizona, New Mexico, the Seri-land of Tiburon Island in Old Mexico; east to Louisiana, Alabama, Mississippi, Florida; then north to the Carolinas, Maine, Nova Scotia, Quebec; west to Ontario, northern New York; thence to end with the Eskimos who, though they are not truly Indians, did and still do some weaving of baskets.

This organization does not mean that basket weaving followed this order in developing.

Maps will be used at chapter headings to aid the reader in locating the area under discussion.

The illustrations will be current and they are photographs by the author of baskets in museums and private collections. Attempts will be made to point out differences of baskets of different areas when discussing plates.

An objective of this volume is an attempt to save from destruction baskets which have been relegated to the back shelf of the garage or to a dusty corner of an attic. "Aunt Susan's" sewing basket which may become yours at her demise must be saved and cherished as the art work of the original American. Too many times this basket is not recognized and is discarded. This is nearly as cardinal a sin as using a fine canvas to start a fire.

If using this volume makes it possible for the reader to recognize one Indian basket in a lifetime and preserve it for another lifetime, then I will feel a sense of accomplishment.

When I acquired a small accumulation of Indian baskets in 1955, my curiosity was sharply aroused and many questions began demanding answers. I thought it would be a simple matter to go to the library and find the answers, but I was disappointed. After quite some search and inquiry I found few books covering the subject of baskets in print. Good information was very difficult to obtain.

Several years of searching came up with much fine information, although much of it hidden in great stacks of other material. I became aware that information about Indian basketry was not to be easily found by the casual collector. Visits to museums and to private collections usually ended in confusion, due to inadequate classification or classing so fine that the place of any basket in the over-all picture was lost.

Since the turn of the century, writers have bemoaned the fact that Indians were no longer weaving fine baskets and I must echo their findings. It is true that we must preserve what we now have for there is to be no replacement, just as there is no replacing a fine Rembrandt or Renoir.

There are, however, some Indians who continue to make an effort to weave. Some, such as the Papago, do quite well and have developed some beautiful baskets for sale. Other areas where a few baskets are made include Alaska, the northwest United States, Louisiana, Florida, North Carolina, Maine, Nova Scotia and Ontario. I collected a few baskets in these areas during 1967-68. They are all orientated to commerce rather than toward utility or art expression.

To the reader who now wonders if it is still possible to make a fine collection, the answer is "yes." One beautiful basket preserved and cherished is a worthwhile accomplishment. A basket from each of the basket making areas, or what we might call a "type" collection, is a real collector's achievement. From this point on, only one's knowledge and pocket money are the limiting factors. Searching for and recognizing a real Indian art is the challenge, and preserving it for always is the great satisfaction.

The question of preservation is of prime importance and I will touch on it here. In the past many techniques have been advanced to preserve baskets, some good and some bad. From my experience of seeing and handling thousands of baskets in museums and private collections; I have arrived at the conclusion that the best procedure is to properly clean a basket by washing in lukewarm water (in a tub) using a mild soap and brushing with a clean one or two-inch paint brush. Then rinse out all soap and place on paper towels to dry. Do not place in sun while drying. Your basket may be displayed in any cabinet or plastic container for all to admire. It should not be handled too much and only with tender loving care.

Many baskets have been varnished by collectors, but I do not advise this procedure as the varnish always darkens the basket in an unnatural way and it tends to lose its natural beauty.

A little insecticide spray in the storage cabinets will protect against any wood eating insects. Keep baskets away from cooking areas and dust areas unless in a proper container. You would not hang your Renoir in the kitchen or the garage. Careless handling of baskets probably destroys as many baskets as the discarding of them. They should not be grasped by the edge or rim, but should be totally supported. Age and dryness tends to cause brittleness of many basket materials and, even though many of them were made for rugged use, they may be broken by carelessness.

Nearly all materials used in basket weaving were woven in moist conditions and an environment of moisture is favorable to longevity. Always avoid mildew by keeping adequate circulation.

When a basket has been properly identified in your collection it should carry an identification marker for the rest of its life. Cloth laundry marks, attached by a thread loop, through any opening in the weave, is one good procedure. The tag should be placed so it does not detract from the design or beauty of the basket. It is impracticable to attach the entire history to any basket. Therefore, a collector should always keep a record book giving as much information as is known about each basket. You may know many interesting things about a basket which should be passed along to others; such as, where collected, when made, by whom, for what use, why given away or sold and what you gave in exchange or cash. Each basket should be recorded accurately, others cannot read your mind.

Recognize Indian basketry as the beautiful art form that it is and cherish all you may find, and your collecting shall know no bounds.

The maps used in this volume show the areas occupied by different Indians before white man disrupted their native cultures. They are prepared from several informational sources:

> The Eleventh Census (Indian) 1890, by U.S. Department of the Interior.
> Report of the U.S. National Museum, 1902.
> The Bureau of American Ethnology, Bulletin 78, 1925.
> The Bureau of American Ethnology, Bulletin 41, 1919-24.
> American Archaeology and Ethnology, Volume 38, University of
>   California, 1939.

The crowding of several different cultures into one reservation area and the complete disappearance of some families or tribes makes the maps obsolete if one attempts to use them for location of a specific group today. The maps will help to locate the area of a basket maker's home-grounds at the approximate peak of their culture. Some of the areas, such as those of the southwest, may closely approximate the original home-grounds.

The illustrations used are photographs by the author. The arrowhead and identification card in most photographs is one inch by two inches. The larger spearpoint in some photographs is two inches by six inches.
Credit for the source will be noted as follows:

R.M.M.—Riverside Municipal Museum, Riverside, California.
B.M.M.—Bowers Memorial Museum, Santa Ana, California.
P.G.M.—Pacific Grove Museum, Pacific Grove, California.
F.L.C.—Frank Lamb collection.
J.C.C.—Jerry Collings collection.
E.C.C.—Ermina Campbell collection.
A.S.M.—Arizona State Museum, Tucson, Arizona.
C.R.I.T.—Colorado River Indian Tribes Museum, Parker, Arizona.
T.P.C.—Ted Ponting collection.
F.E.C.—Florence Eddy collection.
J.S.C.—Mrs. John Slater collection.

BASKET WEAVING AREAS
OF
NORTH AMERICA

The Weavers

From the very beginning of human culture it became apparent that man in order to subsist had to learn to fabricate tools and utensils or be overpowered by other animal forms. When man realized that weapons were necessary to compete and provide food, they designed and built from materials at hand. Women, when they realized that they needed to carry more than they could hold in their two hands, had to design some thing to assist and the most natural thing was to use any pliable material at hand to shape by twisting together a bag or container of even the most simple form. This lot of design fell to women because they were by physical restriction unable to compete with man in his pursuit of game and because they had full responsibility for the raising of offspring and were not allowed to range far afield from such homes as they might have. It became, by natural selection, their duty to do any weaving of materials into forms to aid in storage or carrying. Thus, it has always been the work of women of aboriginal peoples to do the designing and fabrication of baskets.

In some cases the men helped with the gathering of materials to be used for the weaving. Usually this was accomplished by traveling to areas where special grasses or shrubs grew and these were harveted at only a certain time of the year when they were pliable and plentiful. Roots were generally gathered in the early summer when rains or floods had softened the earth. Grasses and barks had to be sought out while the life fluids were plentiful, else they would be too brittle for use. Many times the entire family would camp in an area for several days, gathering. The men did help but it has been reported that the women regularly gathered twice as much as they. The women always did the caring for and carrying of all materials. Often the gathering grounds were many miles from home base.

Special materials were gathered to provide color and decoration for the finished work of aboriginal art. The designs were always women's work, even as today women work designs into their knitting or sewing. In the early work none except natural dyes were used and they required much work and great ingenuity to accomplish. Some materials were prepared and buried in special places to dye, sometimes as long as three months. These early efforts resulted in surprisingly permanent colors.

The most permanent of colors used in weaving, however, were those which occurred in nature, as the blacks of martynia (devil's claw) or the stems of maidenhair fern and bark of redbud. How some of the bright colors, which have lasted for a hundred years or more, were accomplished is still truly unknown.

When we consider all the effort, skill and knowledge required of these early Indian women to provide for their life, small gems of beauty, it is necessary to classify them as true artists. Every possible variation of stitch and weave have been seen in aboriginal basketry, and it has been said that there is not a stitch or turn of weaving today that did not have its counterpart in a primitive basket.

Bert Robinson, who spent the greater part of his life as a government employee among the Indians of the southwest, in his book *The Basket Weavers of Arizona* says, "The weaving of baskets is probably the oldest of the textile arts known to mankind. No race or continent, however, can lay claim to the origin of this art, for it has been worldwide in its distribution. It seems to have been one of the first steps among primitive people in their advancement toward civilization. In gathering wild fruits, berries, nuts, and seeds, they found need for a container in which to collect these foods and transport them to their homes, so they fashioned together leaves or twigs or reeds, from the fields and marshes, into what we call baskets. Among some people this became a domestic art, and the baskets they made were used in the field or for storage or other household uses.

In America, the weaving of baskets has been given a place among the fine arts. The American Indian has given to the world an art that is unique, that is individual to his race; an art that is purely American and one in which the beauty and richness of design is such that all Americans have just cause to be proud. The Indian baskets that we see today are not of recent origin, but rather are development of an art that has been handed down through hundreds of years."

Archaeologists have divided the Basket Makers into three main divisions:

1. *Basket Maker I*—Dating from 1500 to 3800 years B.C. Roving nomads. No definite home. Few specimens of this age have ever been found.

2. *Basket Maker II*—Several centuries later—cave dwellers, and in the dry caves of the southwest, fragments of their baskets have been discovered. Their technique was so well advanced that we are sure of the existence of a Basket Maker I period.

3. *Basket Maker III*—A much later period—up to today—where Indians learned to make homes of a sort, practiced some agriculture and discovered a way to make pottery.

It is true that in all the world there are only basically three principal types of basket weaving.

The first, which includes checkerwork, wickerwork, and twilling, is essentially a cloth weave made free hand in coarse materials. The basis of it is the simple in-and-out weave. That is to say, a single cross strand at a time is worked over and under the longitudinal ones. This type is most easily shown by illustration of the checker-work.

Checker-work

The illustration above shows the bottom of a basket made by Indians of the Nootka Group. Entire baskets are not commonly made this way. The wicker-work of the Hopi Indians of Arizona and the twilling of the Coushatta Indians of Louisiana are examples of this first type. A close examination of their baskets will show that no twining technique is involved.

The second type is twining, which occurs in many varieties, all of which have in common the fact that two or more cross strands are introduced at the same time. This involves the fact that besides being worked in and out among the longitudinal elements, they must also be twined among each other; hence the name twining.

Twining

The changing of direction of twining or the addition of a third strand is commonly used as a means of decoration without addition of a different material or color. A third strand is used also, often introduced on the bottoms of baskets for extra strength and greater wearing quality.

The third process is that known as coiling and, as has often been pointed out, is in strict accuracy a process of sewing rather than weaving. The foundation elements are wrapped or lashed together and this can be done only with the aid of an awl or needle. There is no set of parallel warps to serve as a basis, but the foundation strands or rods coil in a continuous spiral.

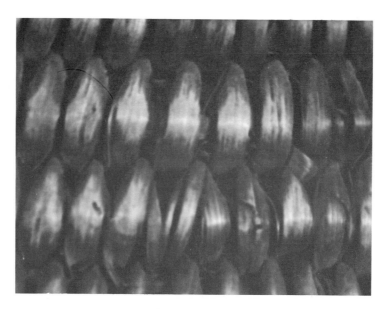

Coiled

Basket weaving seemed to have developed independently in numerous areas among the basket making peoples. When Christopher Columbus landed on American shores all indications were that the Indians of the eastern country had long used baskets and much later when explorers visited the west and northwest they traded for fine basketry and matting. The fineness of the work and high degree of development of form and decoration leads us to believe that already the practice of weaving was hundreds or even thousands of years old.

The baskets shown and discussed in this volume will in general be those which a collector might see and have a chance to acquire. Some exceptions will occur where showing and discussing a rare and inaccessible basket serves the purpose of better understanding the subject.

ALASKA BASKET MAKERS

AREA MAP

The Aleuts

If one holds strictly to the Bering Straits land bridge philosophy of settlement of the Americas, then the Aleutian Indians would only be on the first step of migration to this continent. They survive and have built their culture on some of the bleakest land in the world, cold, wet, fogbound and with little vegetation.

They utilize driftwood and burrow in the ground, in combination, to build a home for themselves. Is it any wonder these women sought to create something of beauty, even as our women of today strive toward some art form. The basketry of the Aleutian women stands out as some of the finest weaving of all. The only source of weaving material being the beach grasses and a type of wild rye. These grasses were split to almost thread size and woven to approach an appearance of fine cloth. Being limited for decorative materials, they learned quickly the beauty of varied techniques of twining to produce a pattern. Later, after contact with the Russians and others, they quickly learned to use an overlay (false embroidery) of worsted materials from any possible source. The designs are usually simple straight lines or squares, but some baskets show small flower forms done with considerable artistry. (Illustrated)

These baskets are quite flexible and most fold quite easily, especially when wet. Thus, when carried empty, they take up little space, yet do yoeman duty in carrying a load home. Many are modest in size and are used for storing personal articles. A form of later years was a two-part wallet for carrying cigars or glasses. World War II brought so many United States GI's to the Aleutian Islands that the culture of the Aleuts has completely changed and very few baskets are now made. The surplus of an army in occupation changes many things, leaving gas cans and assorted empty boxes to be used for carrying and storage. Perhaps one of our GI's left his knitting needles or paints and all art forms will not be lost to the Aleutian Indians.

(A) *A basket of very fine twining weave has a design of worsted material. The basket shape and decoration are the result of contact with the United States or Russian explorers or traders. Material is fine split grass of natural straw color.*

Size: Base-4 in. dia.

Ht.-5" flare to 7".

R.M.M.

(B) *This is a close-up view of the preceding basket showing fine detail of Aleutian weaving. The embroidery is not a grass; a worsted material is used. The Aleut weaving is very fine and flexible, like no other among all the Indians. Usually a small blocked design is used. See other plates.*

R.M.M.

(C) *Here we see open twining with looped border braided to finish. The design is more typical of Aleut weaving. The material used is grass.*

Size: Base-4" dia.

Ht.-9" Rim-10" dia.

R.M.M.

(D) *This basket resembles the previous one, but shows a variation of the twining to create a design and lacks the looped and braided border. Worsted material is used for decoration.*

Size: Base-7" dia.

Ht.-8"

R.M.M.

Aleutian Baskets

(A)

(B)

(C)

(D)

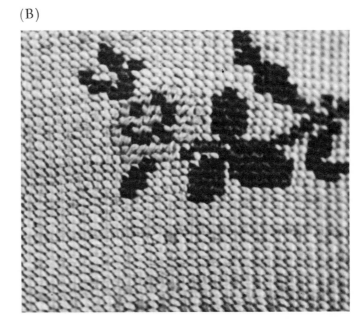

— 13 —

(E) *This is a two-part fitted pouch probably a copy of a glass carrying case or possibly a cigar case. It is of very fine weave and beautifully designed, showing a variation of twining and also using embroidery.*

Size: 2½" wide x 5½" long.

R.M.M.

(F) *Open weave twining with looped border, braided. In addition this has a braided handle or bail. The Aleutian baskets are usually pliable, giving the feel of a stiff burlap, and they may be folded flat.*

Size: Base-13" dia.

Ht.-14". Rim 13" dia.

R.M.M.

(G) *This covered basket is an unusual type used for personal storage of small items. It is beautifully woven and designed. The knob on the lid is a continuation of the weave and not an attached extra.*

Size: Base-5" dia.

Ht. to lid 4½".

R.M.M.

(H) *Another basket with looped and braided border. There is a little variation of the open twining. It is tastefully decorated with worsted.*

Size: Base-8½" dia.

Ht.-10½". Rim-10".

R.M.M.

Aleutian Baskets

(E)

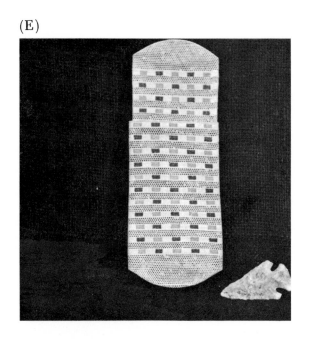

(F)

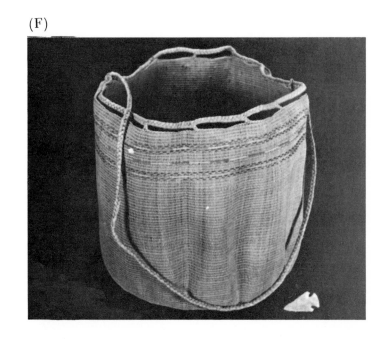

(G)

(H)

Tlingits

The Tlingit Indians occupied the long extension of southeastern Alaska reaching from the Copper River to Dixon Entrance. They had developed a high degree of skill and artistry long before trading ships touched their homeland. They lived on the great shelf of land between mountain and sea.

The Tlingit Indians gathered the roots of the spruce tree to weave a very beautiful basket, decorating with false embroidery by using fern stems and dyed grasses. Alder bark, blueberry, hemlock bark and wolf moss were the natural materials used to produce their colors. These materials were to be found in abundance and it was common practice to use urine as a mordant to set the dye. Copper oxide was also used occasionally to produce a beautiful blue-green color.

The usual weave was close twining, although variations in twining produced beautiful patterns and open work. The false embroidery varies in pattern considerably, producing frets, triangles, crosses and blocks. Occasionally the swastika is to be seen. It would be interesting if we could relate the swastika of this area with that used by the Pima Indians of Arizona, but I have found nothing to indicate that these forms have any cultural relation.

The baskets of the Tlingits were in great demand by traders and, in order to produce greater numbers, the size of baskets was reduced. Rarely do we see any baskets larger than twelve or fourteen inches in any dimension. The fine thin-walled baskets were used for cooking food. They were placed on the ground and sand or soil built up around the outside to support them while hot stones were placed inside in the food mixture.

The Tlingits were masters at making a basket with a rattle top. A double weaving was used in making the basket lid and a void or chamber was left between the

(A) *A common form of basket among the Tlingit weavers. This tapered side open basket is often seen. It is twined with fine spruce root. The design is false embroidery.*

Size: 5" x 7" high.

9" wide.

R.M.M.

(B) *Close-up detail of the twining and false embroidery of (A). The dark design is of glossy fern stem. The other embroidery materials are dyed grasses. The design is not seen on the inside of the basket (hence false embroidery).*

(C) *A small rattle top trinket basket with design in false embroidery of dyed grasses in colors of blue, purple, orange, red, yellow, black and green. An old basket, but probably made for trade or sale.*

Size: 3½" wide x 4" deep.

F.L.C.

(D) *A tapered basket with beautiful design in false embroidery of black, yellow and red. Note the four lines around the basket which are three-strand twining used to strengthen the sides.*

Size: 7" wide x 5" deep.

4" base.

B.M.M.

Tlingits

(A)

(B)

(C)

(D)

Tlingits (Continued)

weavings. In this space they placed small pebbles from the gizzards of geese. When the basket was moved, the pebbles made a small noise. Lead shot was used in later baskets instead of pebbles.

The spruce root baskets are not heavy or rugged. They should be handled carefully for they become brittle when dry and can be easily broken.

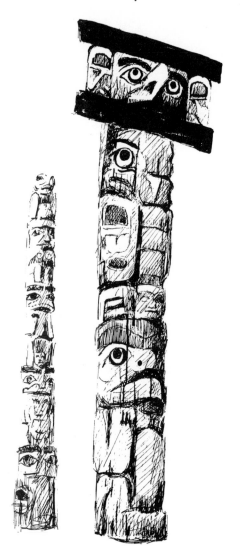

(E) *A fine rattle top basket of twined spruce root with design in gold, yellow, and brown. Probably used as storage for personal items.*

Size: 6½" wide x 5" deep.

F.L.C.

(F) *This trinket basket with handle was probably made for sale. Note the open work. The eye holes are accomplished by crossing the warps and twining the crossovers. The false embroidery is of black fern stem.*

Size: 3½" wide x 4½" deep.

R.M.M.

(G) *Spruce root as a twining material makes a very smooth finished basket. The walls are not thick and are flexible. False embroidery which is entirely on the outside of the twining weft is very adaptable to variation of design.*

Size: 5½" to 8" wide.

      6½" deep.

(H) *Showing quite some variation in decorative design, this colorful basket is finely twined of spruce root. The false embroidery is black, red, yellow, green and orange. This basket is almost a pure cylinder in form.*

Size: 12" wide x 10¾" deep.

R.M.M.

Tlingits

(E)

(F)

(G)

(H)

Haida

The Haidas occupy the Queen Charlotte Islands located off the coast of British Columbia. They were not noted as great basket weavers, but rather as makers of hats.

The hats they produced were very desirable items of trade with early day traders of the area. The weaving techniques and the use of the spruce roots as a material were probably learned from the Tlingits to the north.

Their weaving technique was twining with variations to produce a very pleasing effect. They painted on a design, usually in red, black and green. These designs were traditional and symbolized some natural object or event. The use of the eye as a principal part, used with variation, could tell many different stories.

The Tsimshian Indians of the mainland made a hat indistinguishable from that of the Haidas.

The painted basket of the Haidas is only rarely seen, but can be as beautiful as the hat. Other baskets of the Haidas depended on a variation of the twining to produce a very subtle design.

(A) *The Haida hat twined with spruce root. Variation of the twining produces a fine under pattern for the painted on designs of black, red and blue-green. The designs were often idealized forms of the raven or bear and probably had totemic significance.*

Size: 13" wide x 8" deep.

R.M.M.

(B) *An unusual Haida twined basket, larger than most, and with painted on design. Probably a ceremonial basket. Design is painted in black and red.*

Size: 8½" wide x 10" deep.

A.S.M.

(C) *A spruce root twined basket of the Haidas with a false embroidery in plain straw color. The technique copies the Tlingit weaving.*

Size: 12" wide x 9" deep.

R.M.M.

(D) *This cylindrical basket of the Haida has no false embroidery. The design is merely a darker strand of spruce root introduced in three bands around the basket. Note the variation of weave around the top section. This is a common technique.*

Size: 6¾" wide x 7 deep.

R.M.M.

Haida

(A)

(B)

(C)

(D)

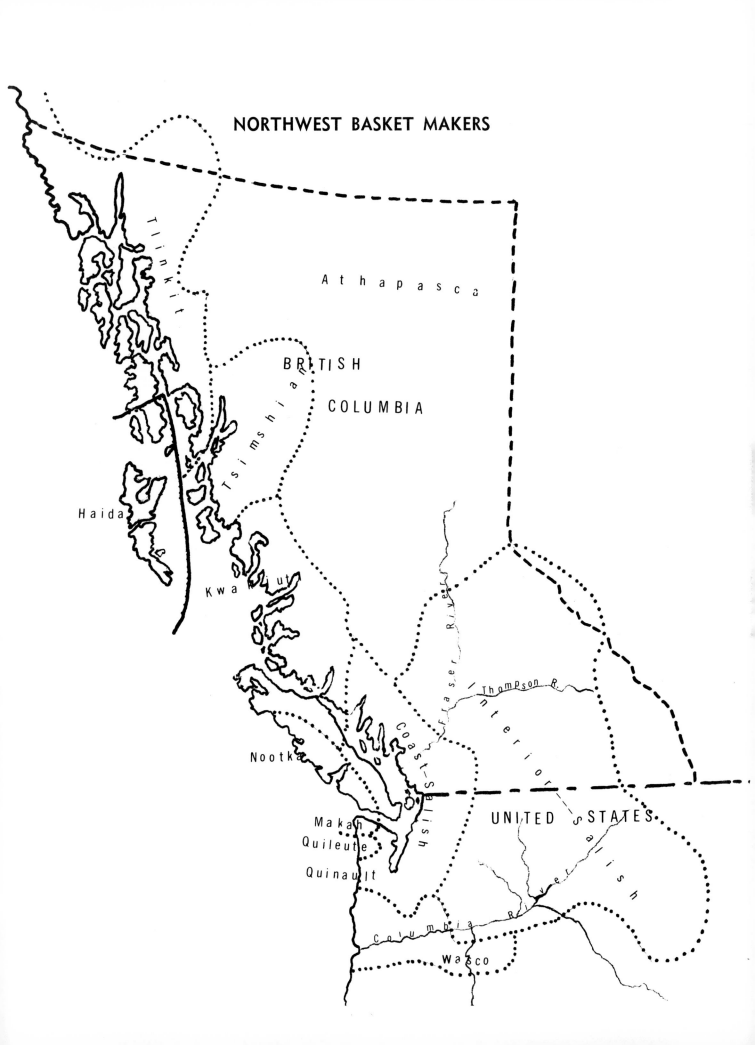

NORTHWEST BASKET MAKERS

Tlinkit

Athapasca

BRITISH

COLUMBIA

Tsimshian

Haida

Kwakiutl

Coast Salish

Fraser River

Thompson R.

Interior Salish

Nootka

Makah

Quileute

Quinault

UNITED STATES

Columbia River

Wasco

Salish Group

The Salish Indians originally were at home in a large area of the northwest country, extending from the Columbia River to the upper reaches of the Frazer and Thompson Rivers of British Columbia and from Vancouver Island to Idaho. In most studies of this group it is divided into the Coast Group and the Interior Group. This division still applies to some degree in considering basketry.

To help avoid confusion to the collector it is well to pause here to explain that this is a very large group with many subnames, such as: Thompson River, Lillooet, Cowlitz, Chilcotin, Frazer, Spokane, Squamish, Snohomish, Nisqualli, Chehalis, Clallam, Wenatchi, Columbia, and Okanagan. In Franz Boas' report of the Salish dialects in 1800, he gives 38 names. Kroeber, in 1939, gives approximately the same number. These groups are all related linguistically but cultures vary greatly from the plains country to the Pacific Coast and from the Columbia River valley to the upper Frazer River. The basketry of the Salish is greatly dependent on the red cedar and its distribution. Thus, the baskets seen existing today are usually from areas of the great river valleys (Frazer and Thompson) and from lesser valleys along the Puget Sound.

In the Salish we see an example of coiling technique and they use it in two forms: coiling over a cedar splint with red cedar root and coiling over a bundle of fine roots or grasses. The use of the splint made a rigid form and was useful as a pack or burden basket. The use of the bundle made for a tighter weave and was better for use as a cooking basket. The fibres would swell with moisture and become water-tight. Heated stones were placed in this type basket to cook food.

Among the south coastal Salish it was also common to use twining technique to make fish traps and open-work baskets for carrying clams. They made a strong

(A) *This coiled basket of cedar root weft over a root or grass bundle is completely imbricated. The lighter background is straw color and the design is black of fern stem. Note the variegated border which is not uncommon. This is probably a berry picking basket.*

Size: 4¼" to 9" wide.

9" deep.

R.M.M.

(B) *A tray coiled over cedar splints using cedar bark and grasses as the sewing material. This is a modern design.*

Size: 18" x 13" wide.

1¾" deep.

F.L.C.

(C) *A trinket basket finely coiled of cedar and only partially imbricated in black and natural straw color. Note variation of the border.*

Size: 8" wide x 5½" deep.

R.M.M.

(D) *A large burden basket imbricated over-all with reinforcing wood strip around top to which are fastened carrying loops. The colors are straw, dark red and black. Probably Chilcotin.*

Size: 10½" x 14½" wide.

11" deep.

R.M.M.

Salish

(A)

(B)

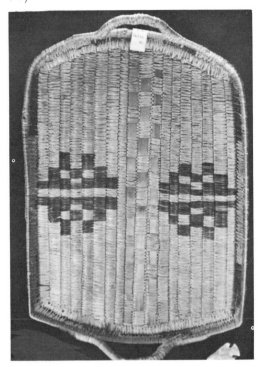

(C)

(D)

Salish (Continued)

carrying bag by the wrapped twining method. A characteristic of this basket was the use of the figure of horse or dog as the design around the top. The twined baskets from the Interior Group resemble the work of the Wasco of the Columbia River area. Twilling was also used to make mats and pouches. The coiled baskets of the Salish were decorated by a process called imbrication which was accomplished by introducing a strip of colored bark or straw to be caught under and folded back on each stitch of the coiling. This imbrication might cover the entire basket or only a portion, but it can be in very pleasing designs and colors. The colors most commonly seen are green, dark red, brown, and natural light straw or yellow. These coiled baskets are quite rugged and many have had a long life.

The Salish made a cradleboard, or more properly a cradle basket, which was entirely coiled and imbricated with beautiful design. They are carried horizontally across the back as opposed to the vertical methods of carrying used by most Indian mothers.

(E) *The personal storage box is coiled over cedar splints and highly decorated by imbricating in colors of red, yellow, brown and black, a prized personal possession.*

Size: 10" x 17½" wide.

7¾" deep.

R.M.M.

(F) *A twined basket with crossed warps leaving an eye hole. This basket could be quickly made, but strong enough to carry a full load of clams or other foods.*

Size: 13" wide x 9" deep.

R.M.M.

(G) *A simple twined basket of coarse grasses and roots for gathering and storage. Alternate materials give a variegated appearance.*

Size: 10" wide x 8½" deep.

R.M.M.

(H) *An example of coiling using a flexible warp. It is a strong carrying bag with braided handle. This basket could be folded flat when empty for ease of carrying. Probably Cowlitz.*

Size: 12" wide x 12" deep.

B.M.M.

Salish

(E)

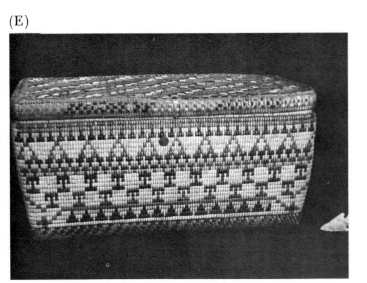

(F)

(G)

(H)

(I) An example of wrapped twining, using the wrap for strength and design. It is a flexible but strong basket. Probably Klickitat.

Size: 7" x 13" wide.

9½" deep.

R.M.M.

(J) Imbricated cooking vessel of cedar roots. Even though this basket was designed for cooking, the maker could not forego decorating it. When collected its designs were lost under cooking residues.

Size: 11" x 9" wide oval x 8¼" deep.

F.L.C.

(K) Trinket basket showing influence of white man. Basket is tapered form with attached base, not an old form, with imbricated diamond designs of black fern stems and straw colored grass coiled with cedar over bundle of grass or cedar root.

Size: 8¼" x 5" wide.

4¼" deep.

R.M.M.

(L) Coiled carrying basket made of cedar splint warp, sewn with cedar, showing imbrication of fern stem to make vertical stripes. A heavy braid is used at border with braided leather for carrying handles.

Size: 8" wide x 15" long x 7" deep.

F.L.C.

Salish

(I)

(J)

(K)

(L)

Nootka Group

The Nootkas occupied the western or ocean side of Vancouver Island and their culture was closely bound to whaling and fishing. The baskets of the Nootka are made of cedar bark and grasses by a technique known as wrapped twining. The grass is a third element and makes a wrap around each crossing of the warp and woof, thus hiding all of the cedar bark. The bottom or start is usually simple checkerwork of cedar. This type of basket can be very beautiful when well done. The decorative designs are influenced by the whaling and other sea orientated activities. Whales, whaling boats and sea birds are often depicted. These Indians were great copyists. One fine piece has been observed illustrating a peacock, possibly from Russian or Oriental contact.

In this Nootka Group of basket makers we cross linguistic boundaries, for it includes the Quinaults and Quileutes and the Makahs. While the Makahs belong to the same language group as the Nootkas, the Quinaults are related to the coast Salish and the Quileutes are entirely different linguistically. In considering the basketry this need not concern us too much. However, when collecting do not fail to record the maker's family, if known. If any distinction of the basket can be made today, it probably would be through consideration of the decorative designs woven into the basket using dyed grasses. The Nootka probably used the whale and whaler design more than the other makers. This observation probably would hold true only for older baskets as weavers today make whatever designs sell best.

The Nootka also made hats which were worn by the men when at sea in their canoes. These were very finely done and one would be a rare item in any collection. Rush and cedar mats were also made by these weavers.

(A) *The wrapped twining is the most common technique of the Nootka Group who used red, orange, purple, blue, yellow and black. All recent colors are analine dyes. The rim is reinforced with a twig coiled on.*

Size: 10" wide x 7" deep.

R.M.M.

(B) *A nice example of a checker-work basket twined at the finish with a braided carrying handle. Two colors of cedar are used in pattern. This is a good utility form and could be quickly made.*

Size: 6½" wide x 8" deep.

R.M.M.

(C) *A form of basket which seems to follow naturally the use of checker-work. (See Cherokee heart-shaped basket). These were used for carrying personal trinkets. The wrapped twining finish completely hides the cedar.*

Size: 8" wide x 8" deep.

R.M.M.

(D) *A simple workday hat well made by wrapped twining. It is easy to wear and good protection from the weather. The design is of black and yellow using fern stem and grasses. Note the three-strand twining near rim and at top.*

Size: 8½" at brim. 7¾" tall.

B.M.M.

Nootka

(A)

(B)

(C)

(D)

Nootka Group (Continued)

(E) *Weaving entirely covers a clam shell with pebbles placed inside to make a rattle. These were used early as ceremonial aids. Later ones were sold as novelties. Note high bowed whaling boat design.*

Size: 4½" x 4½".

R.M.M.

(F) *Empty bottles have been a treasure to Indians ever since their contact with civilization. The Nootka Group did some of their finest basketry to cover the bottles. The sea gull design was commonly used.*

Size: 11" high.

R.M.M.

(G) *A recent basket is seen here using checker-work, twining, wrapped twining and a coiled border. The ducks or gulls in the design are red, purple and green, using analine dyes. This basket was made for sale.*

Size: 10" long x 8" wide.

5" deep.

F.L.C.

(H) *A jar shaped basket with close fitting lid and all wrapped twining technique. Colors of brown, yellow and red are used in the design around the basket. This is an older basket and was probably used to store personal trinkets.*

Size: 5" wide x 2½" deep.

F.L.C.

Map p 48.

Nootka

(E)

(F)

(G)

(H)

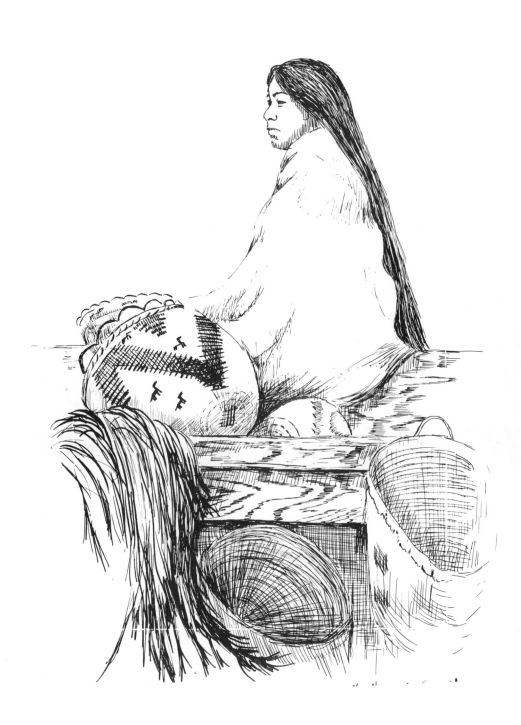

OREGON BASKET MAKERS

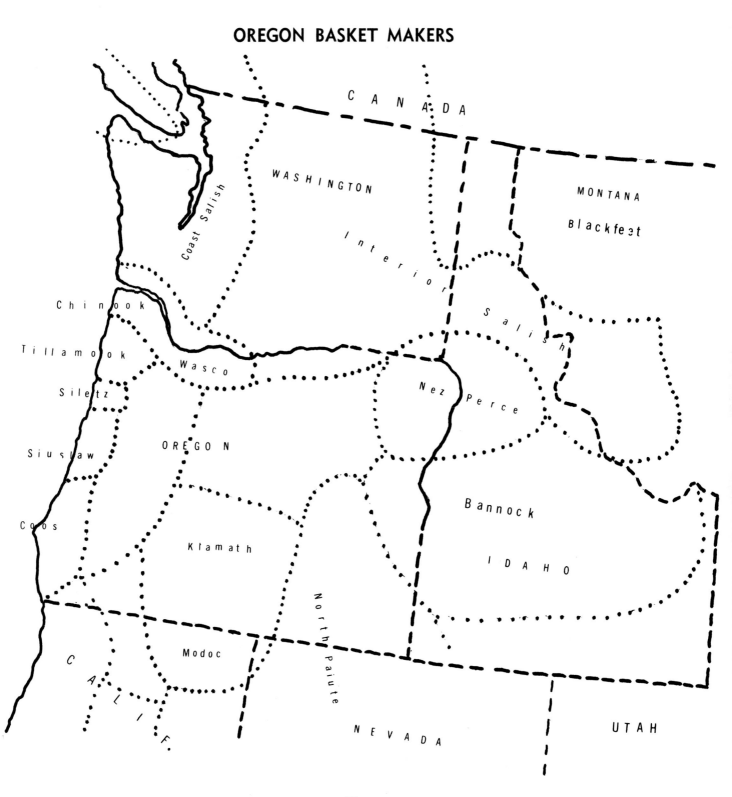

Chinookian Group

WASCO AND CLATSUP

The Wasco Indians of the Columbia River basin near the Dalles are the most important of this group as far as the basket collector is concerned.

They were the makers of the "Sally Bags," a twined basket using both cattail rushes and native Indian hemp. Their designs were done by use of a fiber resembling corn husk, often dyed. These designs were usually of men, dogs, horses, or birds. Some of these forms were idealized and well done. Most of these flexible baskets were bound at the rim with animal skin in older specimens and with scrap leather or white man's cloth sewn on in later baskets.

It is not unusual to find a good "Sally Bag" with a bottom of what is obviously white man's twine.

In 1858, the Warm Springs Reservation was established in north central Oregon. The Chinook, Wasco, Clatsup and other tribes of the area now live on this reservation. Little or no basketry is now done there. Some beadwork is sold to tourists.

The Clatsup, who lived nearer the coast, made mats and wallets of cattail. These are not commonly found today.

(A) *A flexible twined basket of native Indian hemp with a braided handle covered with buckskin. The design is a horse since the tail is down. (When a dog is depicted, the tail is up.)*

Size: 5" wide x 5" deep.

B.M.M.

(B) *A twined "Sally Bag" showing man as a design. A very strong small bag which could withstand heavy use. All of these bags feel as thought they were woven of a heavy twine. In fact, the hemp did make such a twine.*

Size: 4½" wide x 6" deep.

B.M.M.

(C) *A design common to the Wasco is shown here. Squares and triangles adapt well to this weaving material.*

Size: 5" wide x 7½" deep.

B.M.M.

(D) *The use of buckskin on the rim is commonly observed. This weaver added a few trade beads on the skin for decoration.*

Size: 6" wide x 4½" deep.

B.M.M.

Wasco

(A)

(B)

(C)

(D)

Siletz

The Siletz are mentioned here as an example of the confusion to be found in tracing a basket technique to a cultural background.

The Siletz were a small tribe on the coast of Oregon. Their homeland was used as a reservation starting in 1855 and served as a "depository" for many tribal remnants following the Indian Wars in Oregon. The report in the Eleventh Census of Indians by the Department of Interior in 1890 reported thirty-one different tribes living there.

Some baskets were made and sold on the reservation. A type, known as "Siletz," shows up occasionally in collections and should be mentioned. The forms were obviously copied from white man's utensils, such as ornamental vases and carrying vessels. Most of them were done with braided carrying handles. Following this influence probably made the baskets more salable as a usable item. The material was commonly peeled hazel. Some strands were dyed black to work in a simple design.

(A) *The use of peeled hazel made this a strong basket. The double braided handle made it strong enough for gathering fruit, etc. This is open twining over-all, brown color, without decoration.*

Size: 8" wide x 4" deep.

R.M.M.

(B) *Similar to (A) in shape but close twining employed here and decorated by use of a black and a straw colored strand.*

Size: 8½" wide x 5" deep.

R.M.M.

(C) *Closely twined basket with two darker bands encircling as decoration. Notice the heavy braided border.*

Size: 6" wide x 3½" deep.

F.L.C.

Siletz

(A)

(B)

(C)

Nez Perce

The Nez Perce were by location on the very fringe of the basket weaving cultures. They were probably more nearly related to the plains tribes and were one of the earlier groups to make considerable use of horses.

They developed a technique for weaving a very strong and attractive flexible bag. This bag was quite adaptable for carrying supplies on horseback or on foot and was a desirable item of trade among the earliest explorers of the area.

They used fibres of a native hemp to make a string or cord and twined this into flat bags of varying sizes. The colorful patterns or designs were done in the older bags by use of dyed squaw grass. Later bags used the husk of a type of corn as the embroidery material, thus the name "corn husk" bags. After further contact with the white man, colored yarns or even strips of cloth were used for design.

In the older bags a mineral dye from native clay was often used creating a soft pastel color, as opposed to the bold reds, greens and black of later creations.

The Nez Perce also made a fez-shaped cap, somewhat like an inverted deep bowl, twining it from hemp and rushes using a darker portion of the rush to weave in a design.

The Nez Perce bag is a fine addition to any collection.

(A) A Nez Perce bag designed for carrying a load; made from strong native hemp fibers. The design is in red and black. This bag has buckskin sewn on around the opening border.

Size: 16" x 18".

E.C.C.

(B) Reverse side of the same bag (A) showing the tendency of the weaver to make a different design for each side of the bag.

Size: 16" x 18".

E.C.C.

(C) A hat of the Nez Perce twined with hemp fibers. Wrapped twining was used for design. Note the buckskin tie string on top which was used for hanging hat when not being worn.

Size: 4¾" to 7½" x 6" deep.

R.M.M.

(D) A smaller bag used for personal items woven with native hemp using an overlay of grass or husks. Some were dyed blue, green, or black for making a design.

Size: 7" to 8".

B.M.M.

Nez Perce

(A)

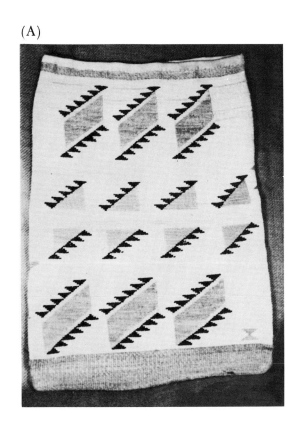

(B)

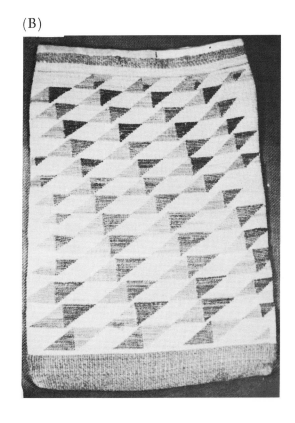

(C)

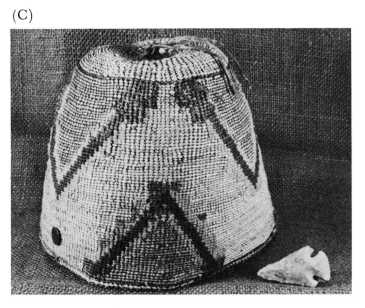

(D)

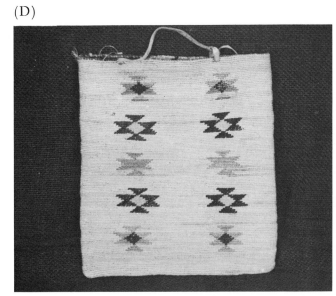

Klamath Group

In south central Oregon the Klamath Agency was formed in 1864 and housed the Klamath, Modoc and a few Snakes from the Snake River region to the eastward.

The Klamath and Modoc had common origin but had lived apart for years. They soon blended their tribes on the reservation and the basketry done is known as Klamath.

Much of their home was marshy and tules grew in profusion. They made flexible baskets, caps and trays. Strands of the tule were twined together to make a strong and flexible material using darker portions, some dyed black in mud springs, to weave in design. Porcupine quills were also used to provide a lighter pattern. The quills were often dyed yellow using a dye extracted from wolf moss by boiling. Other reeds were used to produce overlay patterns. Bundles of tule were bound together to make boats which they used to gather wocus, a staple food item of the marshland. Three-strand twined weaving was often used as a decorative and strengthening means. The finish or rim of the basket often used a turn-back of the warps and braiding with the woof, giving the appearance of a braided border to many of their baskets.

(A) *Klamath hat twined of tule fibers. The design of dyed fibers of the same material. Hats were commonly worn most of the time by the women.*

Size: 7½" wide x 4½" deep.

R.M.M.

(B) *A hat of tule fibers with a three-strand twining used around the crown to add strength. Edge of the cap is braided back to secure ends of weft.*

Size: 8" wide x 4½" deep.

F.L.C.

(C) *A small mat with three-strand twining around outer edge as a stiffener and strengthener twined of fibers of tule.*

Size: 9" wide x 7¼" wide (tray).

R.M.M.

(D) *A gambling mat twined from fibers of tule with dyed strands used for design. The lighter design is porcupine quills dyed yellow.*

Size: 22" (mat).

R.M.M.

Klamath

(A)

(B)

(C)

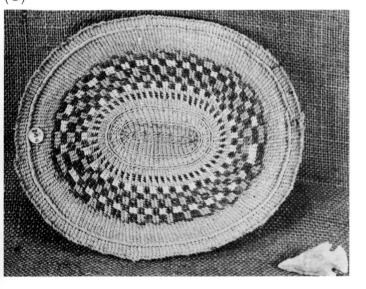

(D)

California Basketry

No other location in all of North America ranks with the area which is now California in the field of aboriginal basketry. This may come as a small surprise to many latter day collectors who are in the habit of searching the states of Arizona and New Mexico for their prizes.

A brief moment with a good map of California and a brief review of its early history makes it easier to understand. The physical features of the state are myriad from the highest peaks to the lowest valleys and from desert to seashore. The usable materials found by the Indian artist were unlimited. The stems and leaves of desert plants, the barks and stems of mountain shrubs, and the grasses and willows of the muddy estuaries were all usable materials. These materials were so diverse that they led to entirely different techniques and types of baskets. Most of the basket making groups made more than one type of basket and used several different materials.

The classic example of diversification was among the Pomo Indians north of San Francisco Bay area, in what is now Mendocino and Lake Counties. They used many different weaving techniques and equally as many different materials. Their accomplishments varied from the crude carrying nets to the finest feathered baskets. Neighbors to the north made an entirely different basket and those not too far distant to the east made again a different form. Part of this difference was due to the materials available, but another factor seems to have been the practice of daughters learning at the knee of the mother. The intermarriage of different families or exchange of women as slaves did blend the basket culture somewhat, making it almost impossible to be exact in identification as to tribe. It is best to hold to the identification of "types" or, as I have chosen, to identify as groups.

The Indians of eastern California crossed state boundaries and it is impossible to talk of California Indians without speaking of Indians of Oregon, Nevada, and Arizona. The great Shoshonean linguistic group covered most of the southern and eastern part of California, extending eastward to cover much of the country as far east and north as Colorado, Wyoming, and Idaho. The northern Paiutes, southern Paiutes, Shoshoni, Monos, Panamint and Chemehuevis are in this group and practiced a similar basket culture, the finest work being coiled. Some of the southern California coastal Indians probably followed a similar basket pattern before the days of the mission. However, the use of different available materials and the influence of the missions developed a type of basketry known today as "Mission Basketry."

The use of native juncas, a weaving material, was carried from mission to mission and a teacher of weaving probably went along much as carpenters and stone masons were exchanged. This led to a general similarity of the baskets. It is possible that this skill was learned from, or developed with, the Cahuilla Indians who never became wholly missionized and, until comparatively recent times, have made some of the most beautiful of the juncus coiled basketry. The Chumash Indians along the coast near what is now Ventura and Santa Barbara made a beautiful basket long before the mission influence was felt. These beautiful baskets are rare and a real joy to see.

The Yuman speaking people of extreme southern California, with the exception of those far inland along the Colorado River, were probably mixed with the Shoshoneans at the mission of San Diego. They did baskets which were essentially the same as those of the mission Indians to the north.

The area of California was in prehistoric times, even as today, a gathering place of many different languages and different cultures. A. L. Kroeber in his *Handbook of the Indians of California* notes seven different linguistic groupings and many more tribal or family names. The organization of basket identification of this great area is at best arbitrary and at this great distance from the source (most baskets of the state were made more than fifty years ago) it is necessary to group according to apparent materials and techniques and designs.

California Basketry (Continued)

The collector who pushes to the frontier seeking original baskets in the California areas is likely to be disappointed for few weavers are left. A few recent baskets can be found on the Hupa Reservation. Very few are to be found in Round Valley and virtually none in Tule Reservation or in the mission reservations of southern California. This makes it doubly important to seek out the lost or unappreciated basket and make a personal effort to preserve it.

The so-called mission baskets will be discussed as a group because their basketry generally follows the same pattern.

The great Shoshonean family of south and east California will be considered in the discussion of the Great Basin basket maker. The Mono, Panamint, Chemeheuvi and Cahuilla were basket cultures of the Shoshonean family residing in California. The Washos, a different linguistic family, lived astride the boundary line dividing California and Nevada and their basket culture was affected by the Maidu who were neighbors to the west, also by the Shoshoneans to the east.

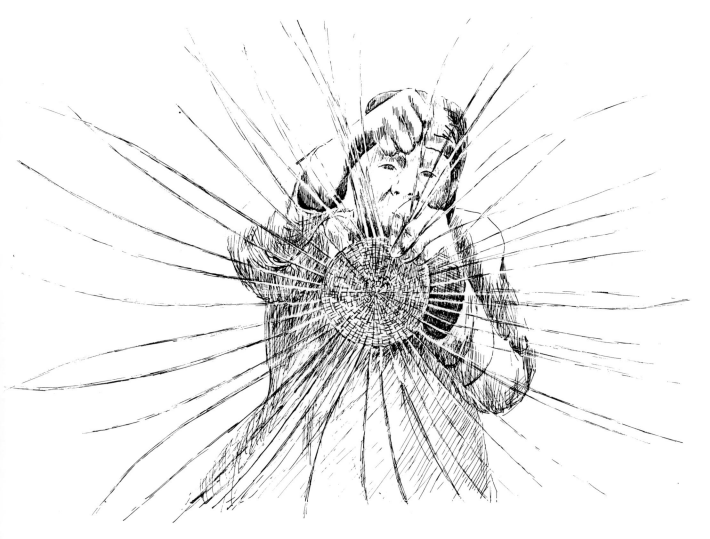

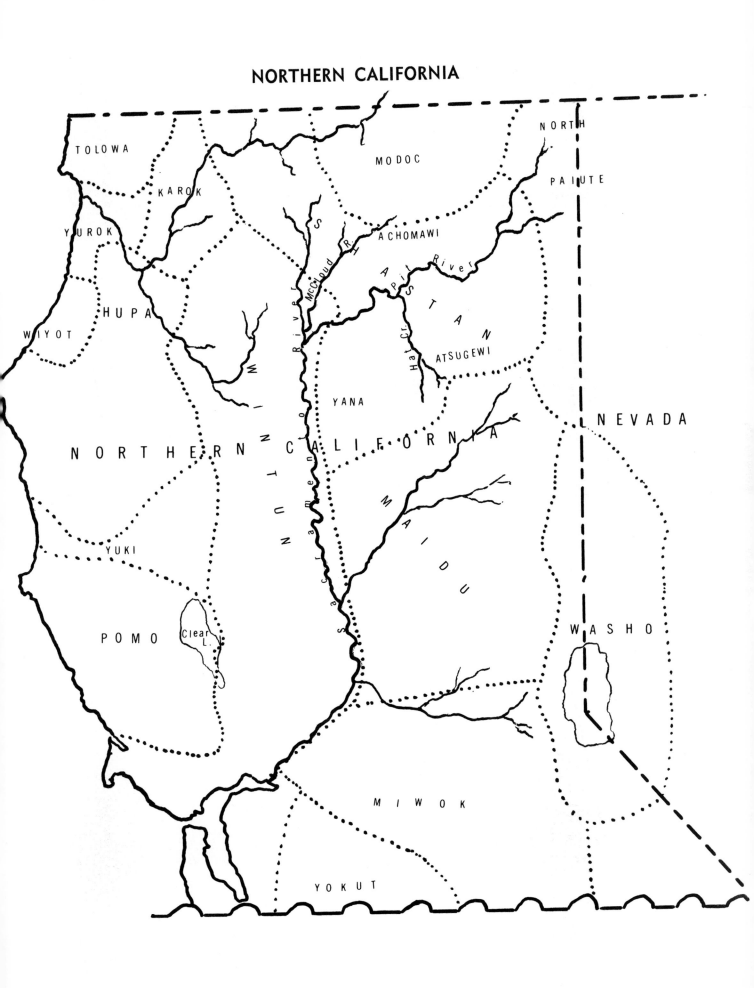

NORTHERN CALIFORNIA

TOLOWA

KAROK

MODOC

NORTH

YUROK

PAIUTE

ACHOMAWI

HUPA

S H A S T A N

McCloud R.

Pit River

WIYOT

Hat Cr.

ATSUGEWI

W I N T U N

YANA

N O R T H E R N   C A L I F O R N I A

NEVADA

M A I D U

YUKI

Sacramento River

POMO

Clear L.

W A S H O

M I W O K

Y O K U T

Hupa (Hoopa) Group

The Indians of California pose a special problem in grouping and in separating for purposes of identification of baskets. We must cross linguistic and family boundaries in many cases.

The basketry of the Hupa Group is such an example. The basketry of the Hupa, Yurok, Karok, Tolowa and Wiyot, and the adjacent Wintun, is all of the same general type, though this group had origins in families or tribes from far different sources. The great factor affecting their basketry seems to be a common usage and availability of like weaving materials. The finely twined hat worn by nearly all of these women and the (usually coarser) cooking bowl were generally of the same weaving technique and used the same materials.

To be able to differentiate one family from another so many years after the basket was woven would be impossible. If the weaver or her lineage is known it is mandatory for the collector to keep this record straight.

Nearly all fine baskets of this group used California hazel as the warp or ribs and the weft was the split root of either sugar pine or yellow pine, using a fine twining technique. The designs were generally solid triangles or variations of the triangle and bands encircling the baskets or hats. These designs were accomplished by two techniques, one was by simply dying the weft strand a different color, and the other was by the introduction of a third element, such as squaw grass or maiden hair fern stems, as a false embroidery. False embroidery is a term applied in early descriptions of weaving in which a design is worked in without allowing the third element to show on the inside of the basket.

Dying of the pine root weft was often done by soaking in a solution made from red alder root. This produced the pleasing red brown color seen in many of their baskets.

(A) *Small storage or trinket basket with hazel warp and pine root as weft. The false embroidery material is squaw grass and fern stem. Geometric designs are common.*

Size: 6½" wide x 4½" deep.

R.M.M.

(B) *A closeup detail of the false embroidery technique. The design material wraps around the external portion of the weft and does not show on the inside of the basket.*

R.M.M.

(C) *A large burden basket. A tumpline was used around the middle diameter of this basket and then over the carrier's forehead when carrying heavy loads.*

Size: 18" wide at top x 17" deep.

R.M.M.

(D) *An openwork basket twined over hazel ribs or warp. False embroidery used as decoration. Rim is a coil over a wood splint.*

Sizes 7" wide x 4½" deep.

F.L.C.

Hupa

(A)

(B)

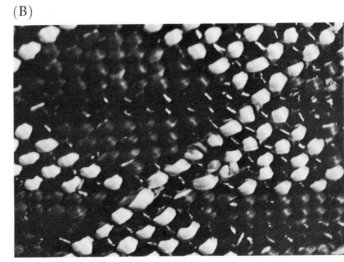

(C)

(D)

Hupa Group (Continued)

Cooking twigs of the Oregon Grape provides a yellow dye used on the squaw grass which was often used as the design element.

(E) *Large storage basket or split pine root twined over peeled hazel nut with fine false embroidery over-all, except the bottom, rim is reinforced with coil over a wood splint.*

Size: 29" wide x 25" deep.

R.M.M.

(F) *Fine basket work over an old Mason jar. (This creates a real problem for a basket and bottle collector. They are both gems.)*

Size: 4" x 7".

R.M.M.

(G) *Unfinished basket showing hazelnut ribs (warp) folded back on themselves. It was not uncommon for early collectors to purchase unfinished baskets for many knew they could not return when the basket was finished.*

Size: 8½" wide x 3¼" deep.

R.M.M.

(H) *Hats of the Hupa were usually smaller than those of some other tribes. The women were smaller of stature. This hat has design of brown which was produced by dying weft with red alder root.*

Size: 6" wide x 3½" deep.

F.L.C.

Hupa

(E)

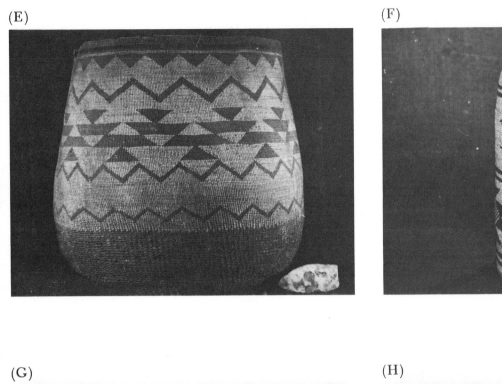

(F)

(G)

(H)

Pomo

The basketry of these Indians, as mentioned in the discussion of California weavers, is undoubtedly the most versatile and diversified of all Indian tribes. They did many designs and shapes using many techniques and many materials. This may seem to be confusing but in spite of the great diversity the form and designs seem to say clearly "I am Pomo." The colors are nearly always a dull red, black and straw color or the brown of pine root. Use of shell beads on the old baskets was common. They made the use of feathers come alive in a symphony of blended colors. The plumes of quail, the red tops of woodpeckers, the yellow of the flicker and the iridescent plummage of others were woven into fine gift and ceremonial basket. They required many months of gathering materials and weaving.

It is reported that most baskets were destroyed during mortuary rites but those that escaped this fate have generally been treasured and preserved by their owners. If you should be so lucky as to acquire or have one be sure to fumigate it often and well to protect it from all elements which would destroy the feathers. These baskets are truly the greatest art of all weavers.

The utility baskets of the Pomo are also beautiful in form and design. The hoppers used in grinding and the carrying baskets are to be treasured in any collection. The Pomo influenced the basket culture of many small tribes around them and any who were capable learned to do baskets which are indistinguishable from those of their teachers.

Today, classification places all of them as Pomo. Among these tribes were the Yuki, Lake and Wappo. It is reasonable to believe that most of the Indians touching on the great San Francisco Bay probably did fine baskets at one time.

(A) *A fine coiled basket. The flare side was common for the Pomo coiled work. They were masters at design as well as at weaving.*

Size: 9½" x 3¼" deep.

R.M.M.

(B) *This large coiled work basket was designed to have heavy use about the Indian home and many lasted for many years. This one shows no such use or wear. Mr. Rumsey collected it about 1908.*

Size: 21¼" x 8¾" deep.

R.M.M.

(C) *A large twined storage basket this size might take more than a year to make. They were used in the Indian home to keep food or other treasures.*

Size: 26" x 17½" deep.

R.M.M.

(D) *Such a large and beautifully made burden basket as this was an important implement of work to the Indian family. It was also a badge of wealth, for it was not easily replaced. The top is reinforced with a half inch wood splint coiled to the edge.*

Size: 26" x 19" deep.

R.M.M.

Pomo

(A)

(B)

(C)

(D)

Pomo (Continued)

(E) A *hopper basket finished with the open bottom so it could be luted to a grinding rock when milling acorns or other foods.*

Size: *17½" wide x 5½" deep.*

R.M.M.

(F) *Another view of* (E) *showing the beautiful design given to even the hardest working basket. Note heavy roll at edge. This is a wood splint coiled in.*

Size: *17½" wide x 5¼" deep.*

(G) *This is a large storage type basket. The warp of hazelnut and the weft of pine root are reasonably heavy in this basket. Its greatest beauty is in its perfect conformation.*

Size: *34" wide x 19" deep.*

R.M.M.

(H) *Winnowing fan used to separate chaff from grain. It is twined with a wood splint completely around the circumference.*

Size: *18" wide x 20" wide.*

B.M.M.

Pomo

(E)

(F)

(G)

(H)

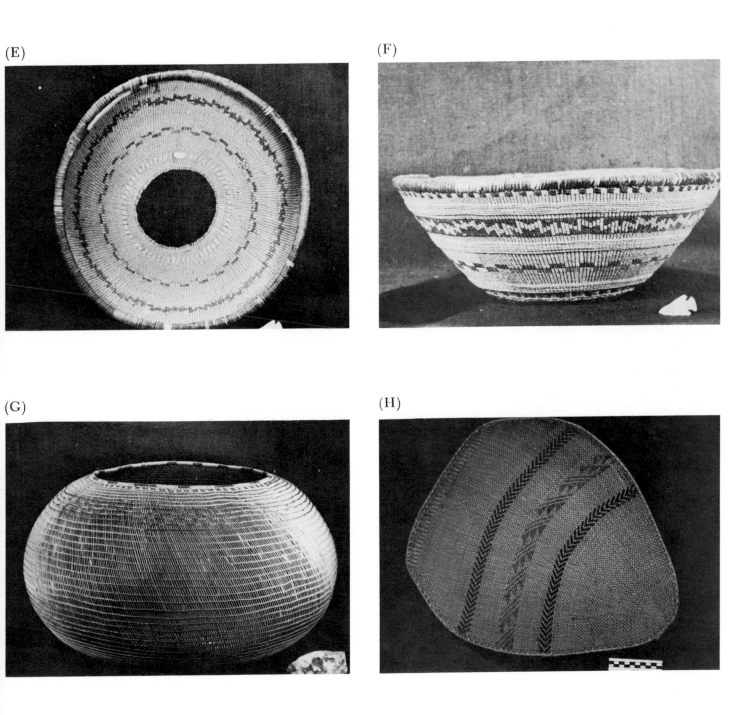

Pomo (Continued)

(I) *Ceremonial basket with fine coiling, partially feathered, quail plumes at rim. Clam shell beads are woven in with the weft. (Not sewn on.) The shafts of the feathers are also woven in with the weft. This type basket was never intended as a utility form.*

Size: 5½" wide x 10¾" long.

      2½" deep.

R.M.M.

(J) *Completely feathered basket, coiled and further decorated with beads of clam shell and abalone (haliotis). These baskets were called "jewel baskets" by early collectors. The feathers of many different birds were used to provide a galaxy of colors.*

Size: 6½" wide x 2" deep.

R.M.M.

(K) *This work basket of heavier material is nicely twined. It would probably last a lifetime in the Indian home being used as a carrying or storage basket.*

Size: 15" wide x 7" deep.

R.M.M.

(L) *A single rod coiled basket. The single willow rod is visible between the stitches or the weft. When evenly stitched this makes a very attractive basket. Various split roots were used as the sewing material and often shell beads were woven into this type of basket.*

Size: 7" wide x 3" deep.

A.S.M.

Pomo

(I)

(J)

(K)

(L)

Shastan Group

The Shastan Group of basket makers cross some heritage boundaries, though not so confusingly as some of the other groups of California Indians. This group includes most of the Indians who were native to the area around Mount Shasta including Eagle Lake and Mount Lassen.

The most common names heard among basket collectors are Pit River, Hat Creek and McCloud River. These were location names for the Achomawi, Atsugewi, Yana and some northern Wintun Indians.

The name of the Pit River was derived from the practice of the native Indians in capturing deer. These Indians dug pits in the trails near the river and cleverly covered them as traps to capture their game for food. This practice was not popular with the occasional stranger traveling these trails who on an occasion found found himself in such a pit.

The baskets of this group are well made and very attractive. Most of their weaving was by twining technique somewhat similar to the Hoopa Group though not so fine. The designs were usually quite different, commonly using what is called a plume or quail topknot. This design progresses upward or outward on the basket and is very pleasing. Many attempts have been made to interpret or put meaning in basket designs. I do not feel capable of such interpretations. I accept most designs as the weaver's personal artful expression.

The materials used varied considerably among this group, which could choose from the shrubs and vines of the mountains to the willows and rushes of the river valleys. A third element was used for making the design. Squaw grass, the bark of redbud, and fern stem were chosen as the usual material for embroidery or overlay of the weft.

(A) *Twined storage basket with hazel stems used for the warp, split hazel or willow for the weft with an overlay or squaw grass making a background of golden color. The design is black of fern stem.*

Size: 14" wide x 8½" deep.

A.S.M.

(B) *Pit River carrying or burden basket. It is conical in shape, twined with an overlay of grass, fern and redbud for decoration. Note the pattern shows on both inside and outside of the basket (not false embroidery). The rim is reinforced with a heavy wood splint. The tumpline (carrying strap) is of native fibers.*

Size: 24" wide x 19" deep.

R.M.M.

(C) *A strong storage or utility form basket with three strand twined bottom for strength. The body of the basket has an overlay over twining with a wood splint coiled to border.*

Size: 8" to 14½" x 11¾ deep.

R.M.M.

(D) *This is a utility basket of lighter material, flexible twining, beautifully decorated with overlay of golden squaw grass and black fern stem.*

Size: 12" x 8" deep.

R.M.M.

Shastan

(A)

(B)

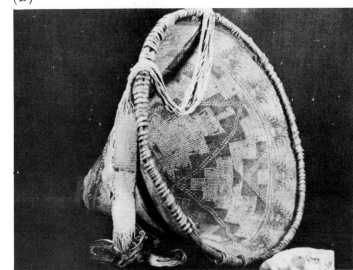

(C)

(D)

Maidu

Immediately south of the Shasta Group was a large area of mountain and foothill country with streams flowing into the lower Sacramento River drainage. In the valleys and along these streams was the home of the Maidu Indians, who were very skillful basket weavers. They did work in both twining and coiling techniques, though probably the best surviving examples are the coiled baskets.

The baskets often were made in the form of a globe, smaller at top than in midsection. The materials used were willow, hazelnut, maple, redbud and the black stem of the Bracken fern. They used the arrowhead, triangle and quail topknot as patterns making a beautiful, shapely and solid basket. The close neighbors of the Maidu were the Washo Indians who joined their territory to the east. The globe shaped baskets were made by both tribes and may be difficult to differentiate, especially since it is known they raided each other's camps for brides. They were quite mixed in marriage and, as has been mentioned, girls learned their weaving at their mother's knee. The materials used vary slightly and design patterns followed local acceptance to some degree. The Maidu basket is usually darker and often carries more dull red of redbud in the design. It is usually close coiled at the border. The Washo basket is lighter in base color with black for design and often uses a diagonal stitch to finish the border. This is another example of cultural similarities in entirely different language groups. One noted difference of the Washo weaving was the prominent use of the single rod coil.

The Miwok lived south of the Maidu and Washo and were north of the Yokut. They shared the basket culture of all three groups. They used the three-rod coiling where they bordered with the Maidu, the single-rod coil where they contacted the Washo, and they are reported to have used the grass bundle where the con-

(A) *Three-rod coiled basket of willow stems, sewn with willow splints and splints of redbud for design. This is a very solid basket with good conformation and design. The gobular form and quail top-knot design are common.*

Size: 8½" wide x 3¾" deep.

R.M.M.

(B) *Coiled shallow tray of willow and redbud. This shape is a common utility form. The ticking on the rim is not common, but shows the good taste of this weaver for it finishes the tray.*

Size: 8½" wide x 1½" deep.

R.M.M.

(C) *This closely coiled globular bowl of willow uses both redbud and fern stem for design making an unusually attractive dark red-black and cream-white finish.*

Size: 9¾" wide x 5½" deep.

R.M.M.

(D) *The bowl shape of the Maidu is a very attractive form and very popular among collectors. It is a strong, long lasting basket if cared for.*

Size: 8" wide x 3¾" deep.

R.M.M.

Maidu

(A)

(B)

(D)

Maidu (Continued)

tact was with the Yokut groups. Some authority today feel the Miwok basketry can be discriminated. They undoubtedly made fine baskets, but I cannot set them apart as a separate basket culture.

(E) *This type bowl probably was used as storage receptacle of personal items. Note the pattern shows on both inside and outside of basket. The outside is the "finish" side of the weave, but the inside is completed with great care.*

Size: 9" wide x 9" deep.

R.M.M.

(F) *Detail of* (E) *showing the fineness of stitch and care with which the design is worked into the coil of the basket. The form shown here is called a quail plume by some collectors. This form and the triangle are popular.*

(G) *A most symmetrical tray coiled of three willow rods, sewn with willow splints and splints of redbud. The star executed in variable forms of the triangle is a difficult pattern, beautifully done.*

Size: 10¼" x 1¾" deep.

R.M.M.

(H) *A utility basket used for gathering and storage, coiled on three rods of willow. The design is of connected triangles done with redbud.*

Size: 17¾" wide x 11½" deep.

R.M.M.

Maidu

(E)

(F)

(G)

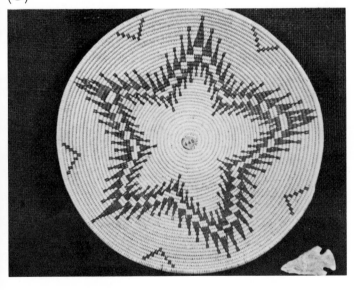

(H)

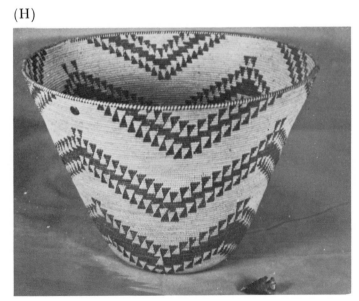

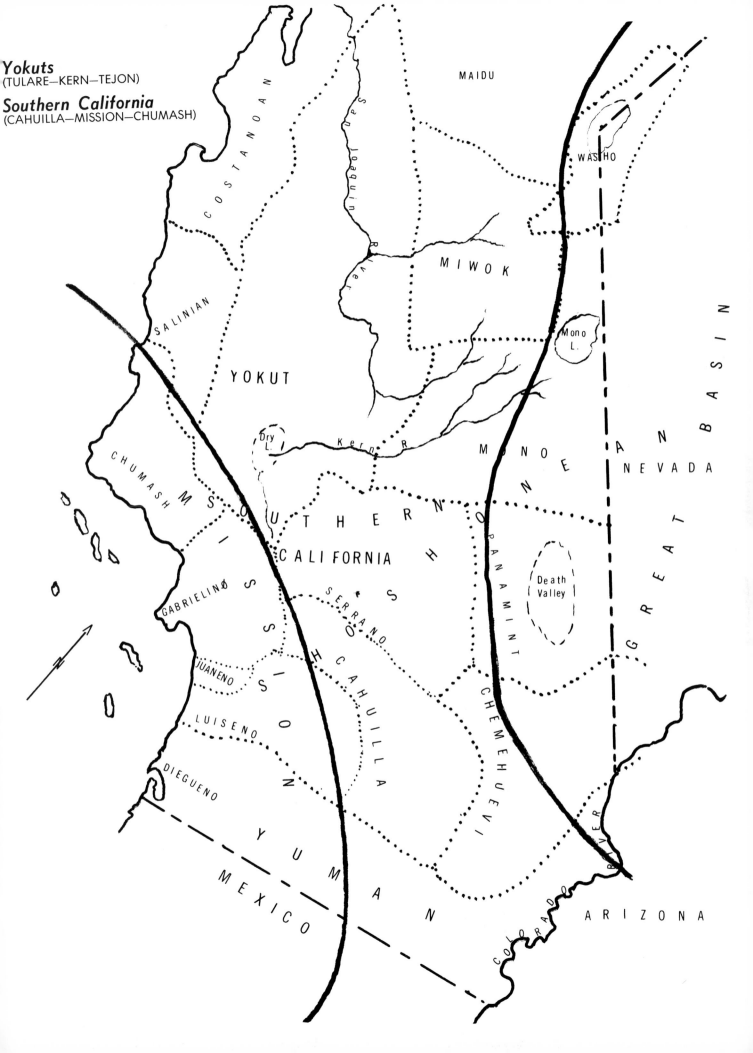

Yokuts
(TULARE—KERN—TEJON)

Southern California
(CAHUILLA—MISSION—CHUMASH)

MAIDU

WASHO

COSTANOAN

San Joaquin River

MIWOK

SALINIAN

Mono L.

YOKUT

GREAT BASIN

Dry L.

Kern R.

MONO

SHO

NEVADA

CHUMASH

SOUTHERN

CALIFORNIA

PANAMINT

Death Valley

MISSION

GABRIELINO

SERRANO

JUANENO

CAHUILLA

CHEMEHUEVI

N

LUISENO

DIEGUENO

YUMAN

MEXICO

COLORADO RIVER

ARIZONA

Yokut

The great central valley of California, occupying both sides of the San Joaquin River for many miles reaching into the Sierra foothills on the east and to the coast range of mountains on the west, was home to another great basket weaving people. These Indians and their culture started a decline upon contact with the white man. Miners in the foothill area and ranchers in the valley crowded them out of their homes, destroying their native cultures. Their basketry in all its fineness and beauty, hopefully, will live forever in the hands of a careful collector. They used almost entirely coiling technique, sewing small bundles of rush or grasses with sumac, redbud, and bracken fern.

The distinguishing design of these baskets is commonly the diamond used in variations and which is said to be copied after the diamondback rattlesnake. The redbud usually makes the diamond in a field of light color and bordered by the black of fern stem. Quail topknot feathers were woven into the weft, forming a fringe or trim around some baskets. This was used in ceremonial or mortuary jars (commonly called bottleneck baskets).

The common names associated with areas of the Yokut weavers were Kern River, Tulare, Tejon and Chuckchansi.

The Yokut boundary to the east was invaded by the more fierce Shoshonean Group and a blend of basket culture is apparent with the Monos and Panamints. Without personal contact with the weavers, which is impossible now, the classification must be by the differences of design. It is practically impossible for a botanist to distinguish between similar materials used, especially after they have been adapted to a basket for more than fifty years. I have spent hours at the microscope and often ended in confusion as far as identification of such material is concerned.

(A) *This unique basket jar was collected by C. E. Rumsey before 1900. It is pictured in Otis T. Mason's* Aboriginal American Basketry, *1902. The basket is now preserved in the Riverside Municipal Museum, Riverside, California. It has a type of coiled openwork called grasshopper weave, the weft "hopping" eight to ten coiled spaces before it again ties to underlying coil.*

Size: 8½" wide x 6½" deep.

R.M.M.

(B) *The bottleneck basket is a virtual trademark of most of the Yokuts, especially the Tulares. The coil is a bundle of grasses. The sewing strand is the root of a marshgrass. The pattern is the black of fern stem and the dark red from redbud. This basket is also called a mortuary basket by some collectors.*

Size: 9½" wide x 7" deep.

F.L.C.

(C) *Coiled jar using willow for coil and as the weft. The design is of redbud and fern stems. This could have been a trinket jar for personal possessions.*

Size: 5½" wide x 3½" deep.

R.M.M.

(D) *Deep bowl-coiled basket with wide sections of dark redbud and black arrows outlined in lighter color. It is a firm utility basket.*

Size: 13¼" wide at rim x 6" deep.

R.M.M.

Yokut

A)

B)

C)

D)

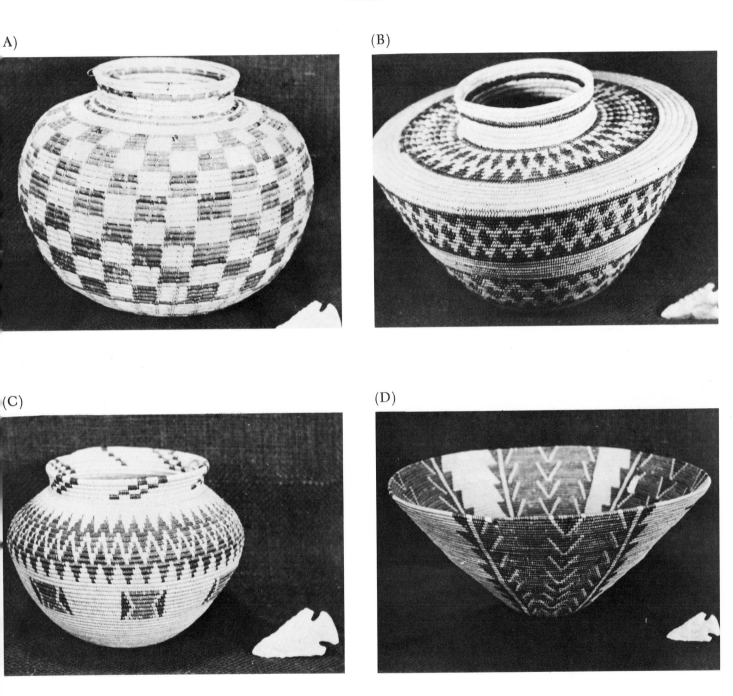

Yokut (Continued)

(E) A very fine coiled narrow-necked basket. It is coiled and sewn with willow, redbud, and fern stem for design. It is a well shaped basket with the finest sewing on any basket this writer has seen.

Size: 9¼" wide x 3¾" deep.

R.M.M.

(F) A feathered bottle neck basket with a rounded shoulder. Quail topknots are caught in the weft at the shoulder. Red and black diamond design is prevalent. (So-called rattlesnake.)

Size: 14" wide x 8" deep.

R.M.M.

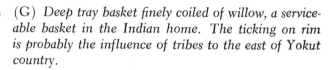

(G) Deep tray basket finely coiled of willow, a serviceable basket in the Indian home. The ticking on rim is probably the influence of tribes to the east of Yokut country.

Size: 15½" x 7½" deep.

R.M.M.

(H) An oval narrow necked basket possibly used for personal trinkets. This basket has very nice conformity and design.

Size: 9" x 5¾" wide x 2¾" deep.

R.M.M.

Yokut

(E)

(F)

(G)

(H)

Southern California   Indian Basketry

(Mission Basketry)

The Indians along the Pacific shores were the first in California to be influenced by contact with white man. When Fra Junipero Serra and Don Gaspar de Portola arrived at what is now San Diego in 1769, a new way of life was about to begin for them. They were to lose almost entirely their native cultures in the process of adapting to the mission way. Probably, only the basket weaving survived without any great change as regarding materials and techniques. Designs were undoubtedly affected greatly after collectors influenced the demand.

Excepting the Yuman on the south and the Chumash on the north, these Indians were chiefly of Shoshonean linguistic stock and closely related to the Cahuilla to the east of them.

The baskets of all these Indians were a desirable commodity to the missionaries and the military men who were with them. Weaving was very likely encouraged in every way possible. When new missions were established, artisans experienced as carpenters, stone masons and planters were sent forth to help in the construction. It is not difficult to conceive that weaving was also on this list of teachings.

The Chumash Indians, who were to come under the influence of five or six different missions, had a weaving culture different from the southern Indians, which was to be converted to mission type in a few short years. Early collectors along the mission routes found baskets which may have had their origin further south, or manufactured at any of the missions where juncus and like materials were to be found.

It is impossible, with rare exceptions, to separate the different mission baskets and they will be considered as a group.

(A) *Twined work basket. This type basket was not often collected, thus not many are to be seen today. They could be rather quickly made and were not so treasured as coiled work.*

Size: 9" *diameter x* 8½" *deep.*

F.L.C.

(B) *A very fine coiled "rattlesnake" basket with the reptile design encircling the entire basket. It is said some weavers feared to use this design as it might anger the snake. The design is of the dark root portion of the juncus.*

Size. 10½" *diameter x* 5" *deep.*

B.M.M.

(C) *A good trinket basket with grass bundle for coil, sewn (weft) of juncus in buff, brown, and black. The black is mud-dyed juncus.*

Size: 8" *diameter x* 3½" *deep.*

R.M.M.

(D) *A recent basket by a southern California Indian weaver using a coil of long fine needles and sewing with juncus leaving spaces so coil may be seen.*

Size: 8" *diameter x* 3" *deep.*

F. L. C.

Southern California
(Mission)

(A)

(B)

(C)

(D)

Southern California (Continued)

The coiled baskets of southern California coastal areas made use of the juncus almost entirely as a sewing material and the coil is usually a bundle of grasses. The stem of the juncus inherently has two colors, a straw color and a brown color. This material was often dyed black by burial in available mud. The devil's claw was available inland from the coast and was used occasionally for black design. These three colors predominate in "mission" baskets in differing patterns. Early baskets were not so highly patterned, using encircling bands with variations. Later baskets, influenced by traders, were more highly decorated, using animal and bird forms, stars, and even some unattractive forms such as lettering. A popular basket depicts the rattlesnake which is a common reptile of this country.

The early Indians of southern California did make and use some ceremonial baskets. A few were decorated with feathers. These forms are not common, nor did they at any time compare with the Pomo feathered baskets. A twined form of basketry was used to make a gathering basket for cactus fruit. These forms used the unsplit whole stem of the juncus with the twining strand often carried over two or three of the warp members at a time. Rarely was any color pattern used in such a basket.

A tray basket, loosely twined, was made for use as a sifter. The burden baskets and the winnowing baskets used by the southern California Indians were almost always coiled.

Cahuilla

The Cahuilla, one of the Shoshonean linguistic families, occupied a great part of southern California. The name Cahuilla is interpreted to mean "master." These Indians were and still are a proud people. They never came under any great influence of the Spanish missions, as did their relatives to the west nearer the

(A) *The medium deep. tray basket was common among the Cahuilla. They were nearly always heavy with design and variegated by use of a good portion of dark juncus in the sewing. The black design was usually of dyed juncus, though some devil's claw was used by an occasional weaver.*

Size: 15½" wide x 4½" deep.

R.M.M.

(B) *Large bowl shapes were used to carry and to store, especially foods such as acorns and grain. The coils would be only slightly larger, yet the basket is rigid and strong. When used to carry, the basket was placed in a net and a tumpline used.*

Size: 20" wide x 9¼" deep.

R.M.M.

(C) *A highly decorated tray coiled with juncus over grass bundle. Animal and insect forms were used for design by some weavers.*

Size: 15½" wide x 4¼" deep.

R.M.M.

(D) *A coiled medium deep tray with design showing a snake charming a bird. It is not too surprising to see the snake copied in basketry among the Cahuilla as the rattlesnakes were common in their homeland.*

Size: 9" wide x 3" deep.

B.M.M.

Cahuilla

(A)

(B)

(C)

(D)

Cahuilla (Continued)

Pacific Ocean. These people had a varied culture which reflected their living in the mountains or deserts, but the basketry they produced generally was of the same type. The use of juncus, a rush growing along streams and lowlands, was used by virtually all weavers as a sewing material. They made mostly coiled baskets using grasses in a bundle for the coil.

The juncus stem naturally presents two colors, a straw color and a pleasing brown color, the brown color coming from the lower part of the stem. To produce a black colored material, the juncus was buried in mud until the desired shade was acquired. However, martynia or devil's claw was not unknown to the Cahuillas.

Early baskets were not so highly decorative, but later ones, to meet the market demand, were a virtual galaxy of color and designs. As a compliment to these weavers, few of their baskets were unpleasing to view and nearly all were well woven.

The task of separating the Cahuilla baskets from those of the Southern California Mission influenced weavers is a hopeless one for it is probable that they all developed their basket techniques much before any Anglo influence.

The Riverside Municipal Museum, located in the center of Cahuilla country, has undoubtedly the largest and finest collection of attributed Cahuilla baskets.

The Malki Museum on the Morongo Reservation, a short distance east of Banning, California, has Cahuilla baskets and displays one of the early grain storage bins.

The Cahuilla also made a twined basket, used as a gathering or utility basket, using the entire unsplit stems of juncus. This basket form was not so popular among collectors and, though there were probably many made, not too many have survived.

Chumash

(Santa Barbara)

Although the Chumash came under mission influence very early, their basketry deserves to be set aside from

(A) *The globular or jar form basket was popular among Chumash weavers. This one is coiled of willow and a dark material for creating a variegated design. The alternate black and white on the rim is usual.*

Size: 6¼" wide x 5" deep.

J.S.C.

(B) *The coiled tray was a utility item with the Chumash. A principal border design was nearly always used three or four coils from the rim. Note the ticking on the rim.*

Size: 8" wide x 1¾" deep.

R.M.M.

(C) *A twined water bottle about one gallon capacity. This was lined with asphaltum to waterproof. Three strand twining was used to add strength and design. A hole has been poked in the basket and lip cut off.*

Size: 7" wide x 8¼" deep.

P.G.M.

(D) *Larger water jar of approximately three gallon capacity. It was twined and lined with asphaltum. Three-strand twining was used for strengthening. When found in a burial cave, the bottle had been made useless by a cut hole at bottom edge and cut section at the neck.*

Size: 10" wide x 19" deep.

B.M.M.

Chumash

(A)

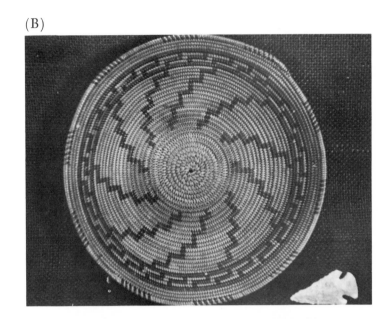

(B)

(C)

(D)

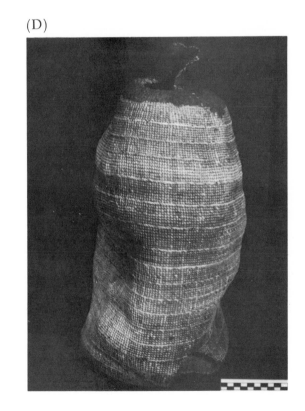

Chumash (Continued)

that of the so-called mission type. The excellence of their work was quite early recognized by Spanish explorers along the coast. It is reported that these Indians brought fresh water aboard the early sailing vessels in containers of woven basketry sealed on the inside with asphaltum to prevent leakage. These bottles were made of willow by twining technique. Some of the early trays woven as gifts to the white people are existing examples of the highest skill in weaving.

The Chumash basket is of fine weave and usually simple design very tastefully done. They liked to use the varied colors of juncus to sew the coils, creating a mottled effect. Besides the dish-tray and water bottle, they also made a low profile olla by coiling. The stitches are generally finer than that of other southern California baskets.

GREAT BASIN

SHOSHONIAN   WASHOAN

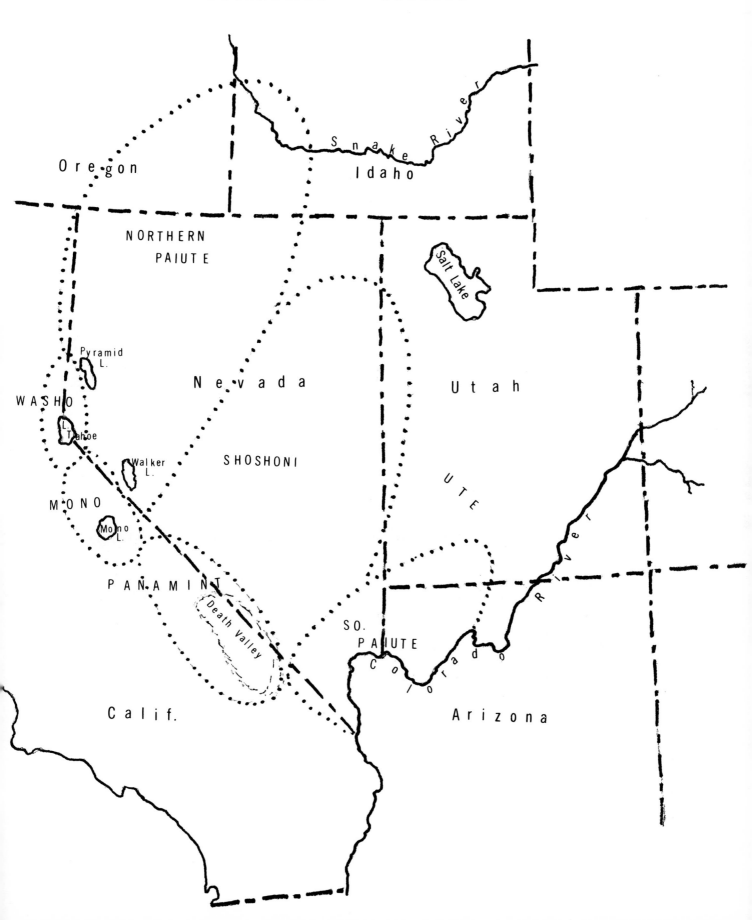

Snake River

Oregon

Idaho

NORTHERN
PAIUTE

Salt Lake

Pyramid
L.

Nevada

Utah

WASHO

L.
Tahoe

Walker
L.

SHOSHONI

UTE

MONO

Mono
L.

PANAMINT

Death Valley

Colorado River

SO.
PAIUTE

Calif.

Arizona

Great Basin Basketry

(Shoshonean)

The great Shoshonean linguistic group of Indians were roaming hunters and gatherers. They rank third after the Algonquin and Athapascan in land area occupied. They were generally confined in their movements to the area between the Sierra Nevada and the Rocky Mountains. This area includes most of the states of Nevada and Utah and parts of California, Arizona, Oregon, Idaho and Colorado. They were not a war-like people. A great part of their activity was utilized gathering enough food to live. Their basket culture was greatly influenced by this need. They made some of the best seed gathering fans and winnowers and their twined conical burden baskets excelled. They also made a coiled basket used in cooking their food. The twined water bottle was a necessity, for they traveled great distances between sources of water. Nearly all groups made hats or caps worn by women. These protected the forehead when carrying heavy loads using the tumpline.

A great many tribal and family names come within this large group. Not all were great basket makers. The northern Paiutes, Shoshoni, Mono, Panamint and the southern Utes all made baskets. The Washos were not Shoshonean but are included in Great Basin basketry. They did share their basket culture. The Cahuillas of California, the Chemehuevi and Hopi of Arizona were Shoshonean family but did not share the same basket culture and are discussed elsewhere.

It is quite difficult to differentiate in much of the basketry of these groups. If one of their water bottles is identified as northern Paiute, it could as easily be identified as Mono, Shoshoni, or Ute and may have been made by any of these groups even though found in use by any other. However, there are some minor differences in other forms of their baskets and it seems right to separate to some degree.

Great Basin Basketry (Continued)

Among the coiled baskets of the Shoshoni the big horn sheep was a popular form to be depicted on baskets. An occasional man form is seen but is not usual. Most of the designs are simple lines, some varied to a continual "V" or "W" around the circumference of the basket.

The northern Paiute did a coiled basket utilizing the single rod for coil and sewing alternately over two coils.

In the early 1900's when Indians from many sources were employed to pick hops in the northwest, the northern Paiutes came in contact with such groups as the Pomo Indians of northern California and greatly admired their feathered baskets. It is noted that many Paiute workers spent most of their earnings to buy such baskets to take home. The beaded baskets of these Paiutes probably followed this Pomo inspiration.

The southern Paiutes were a more sedentary and agricultural group. They did not make too many baskets. The Paiute group and the southern Utes in addition to making the water carrier have for many years made a tray which among collectors is known as the Navajo ceremonial tray. At one time the Navajos made this form for themselves but after the introduction of sheep into their country they excelled in weaving their blankets and rugs and could trade these for baskets to their own advantage. Few, if any baskets, are now woven by the Navajo. Most so-called Navajo baskets are, at the present time, done by the southern Utes who live in southern Utah and are not too far from the Navajo country.

Washo

The Washoes belong to the Hokan linguistic family and are the only non-Shoshoneans included in the Great Basin Group of basket makers. They shared a common tribal boundary with the Maidus, a line generally following the crest of the Sierra Nevada Mountains. They also shared in their basket culture, using much the same techniques and making baskets quite similar in shape, the globe form being popular with both tribes.

They also used similar materials but differed in design; the Maidu generally making a heavier design using more redbud and fern stem. The Washo basket appears usually lighter in color and weight. The coiled Washo baskets quite often are finished at the rim by long diagonal sewing stitch which is not common with the Maidu. The Washo and the northern Paiute did another coiled form of basketry using a single rod or coil leaving the sewing open to display the rod. This form can be quite attractive.

The Washo living more to the east of the mountains made a beautiful winnowing tray, not too unlike those of the Monos and Paiutes which will be discussed later. The basketry of the Washoes was brought to great fame by a great weaving artist, Datsolale. It is reported that one of her baskets sold for $1,500 during her lifetime (early 1900); a greater sales accomplishment than that of most of the old world masters during their lifetimes. It is known that she sold many baskets not of her own making acting as an agent for other good weavers of her tribe.

(A) *Coiled storage basket commonly used to hold grain, fruit or other foodstuff. The coiled baskets of the Washo are outstanding for even stitching and beautiful design.*

Size: 19¼" diameter x 10½" deep.

R.M.M.

(B) *Seed gathering fan twined of willow withes used to sweep seeds from standing grasses into a gathering basket.*

Size: 8" wide x 21" overall.

R.M.M.

(C) *Winnowing tray made by twining technique. A strong willow withe used on entire border for strength. This form used to separate chaff from the grain by tossing in a light breeze.*

Size: 11" wide x 14" long.

R.M.M.

(D) *Twined burden basket. These varied in size according to need and ability to carry. They are strongly made and reinforced with a willow branch coiled to the lip of the basket.*

Size: 17" diameter x 15½" deep.

R.M.M.

Washo

(A)

(B)

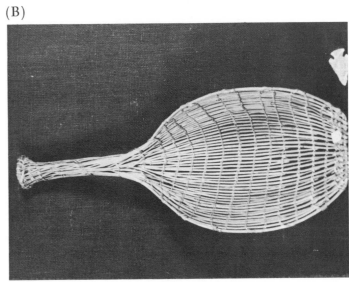

(C)

(D)

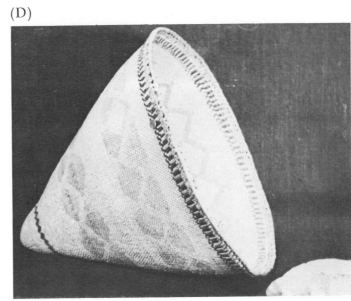

Washo (Continued)

(E) *Fine coiled bowl is a good example of delicate design and symmetry of form. Many of this type basket probably never saw any use but were sold to collectors more profitably. This type of basketry is associated with a famous Washo weaver named Datsolalle.*

Size: 11¼" diameter x 4½" deep.

R.M.M.

(F) *Detail of (E) showing fine stitching. The weft is narrow and the length of the stitch is quite regulated. The material is usually willow for coil and sewing weft. The design is made using the black stem of brake fern or the dark red of redbud.*

R.M.M.

(G) *Coiled deep bowl with a border of false braid. This accomplished by use of one strand only, executed in a figure eight pattern. Few weavers, other than the Washo, used this finish.*

Size: 11" diameter x 6" deep.

R.M.M.

(H) *Globular bowl coiled over three-strand willow bundle. The design was worked with fern stem. Note the false braid at lip of the bowl.*

Size: 8¼" diameter x 4" deep.

R.M.M.

Washo

(E)

(F)

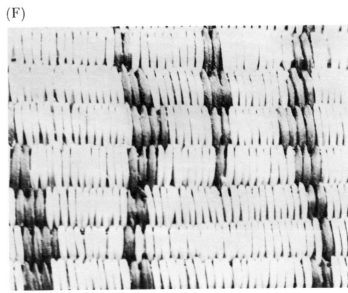

(G)

(H)

Mono

The Mono Indians were a division of the northern Paiutes who were linguistically Shoshoneans.

They occupied semi-arid area east of the Sierra Nevada Mountains in the area known now as Mono Lake. They moved back and forth from mountains to desert with the change of seasons.

They made beautiful coiled baskets using them for storage and cooking. Women's caps, seed beaters, gathering and winnowing baskets were made by the twining method. They also made a water bottle similar to the Paiute using a twining technique and pine pitch to waterproof. These water bottles were in the form of an old fashioned wooden top, pointed bottom flaring to a wide shoulder and closing quickly to a narrow opening or spout at the top. They varied in size from a canteen to be carried on short trips to a large storage size to be left in camp. They were designed so that they could be laid on their sides, balanced so nicely that a child could tip them for water without spillage. Loops of woven hair were often worked in at the shoulder of the bottle to attach carrying straps of buckskin.

(A) *Coiled bowl basket is a common household item in the Indian home. The material of this one is willow with design of devil's claw. The cooking baskets were larger and more closely sewn.*

Size: 8" diameter x 2½" deep.

R.M.M.

(B) *Closely twined carrying jar. If used for water, the basket was saturated with pine pitch to waterproof. This type sometimes was used to store seeds or pine nuts when transporting long distances.*

Size: 11½" diameter x 14½" deep.

R.M.M.

(C) *Seed gathering and sifting basket with open twining over withes of willow as the warp. A reinforced border was coiled on.*

Size: 8" wide x 14" long.

R.M.M.

(D) *Burden basket twined of willow and reinforced with a branch coiled to lip of basket. These were carried on the back with a carrying strap around the midsection of the basket and over the carrier's forehead.*

Size: 13" diameter x 15" deep.

F.L.C.

(A)

(B)

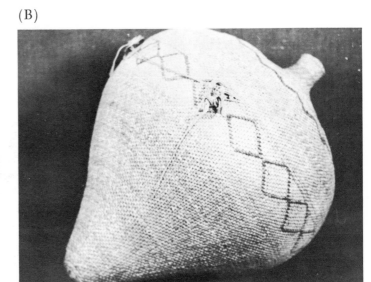

(C)

(D)

Panamint

The Panamints or Death Valley Indians seem to have selected one of the most undesirable areas of the whole world in which to make their home. Probably because of this choice their culture was for many years less disturbed than others. The baskets of this Shoshonean family were very well made and are similar to the Mono baskets in many ways. They also resemble the Yokut forms. The most dependable difference was the use of sumac or willow stems for the foundation of the coils instead of using bundles of reeds. They used the red root of a tree yucca and the black of Martynia pods for color patterns of red and black. They coiled mostly a deep bowl similar to, but smaller than, the Mono or Yokut. A common feature was the alternation of a light and dark strand at the finishing of the rim, sometimes called ticking. The red shafts of the feathers of the Flicker were sometimes used as a small design or signature. They used twining for seed fans, pack baskets and water bottles. The latter was sealed with pine pitch to waterproof.

The water bottles of all the Great Basin weavers were quite similar and they probably were an item of trade among all of the group.

(A) *This coiled deep dish design with figures of horses and arrowheads of devil's claw (Martynia) is a good utility form.*

Size: 6¼" wide x 3" deep.

R.M.M.

(B) *Twined water jug with carrying loops. This shape was not easily spilled by tipping. Pine pitch was used to waterproof jug. Note the three-strand twining for strength visible where pitch is missing.*

Size: 9½" diameter x 10" deep.

R.M.M.

(C) *Unusual rectangle form coiled basket. Several weavers among these Indians made this shape. The big horn desert sheep is a favorite pattern.*

Size: 8" x 5" wide x 4" deep.

R.M.M.

(D) *A single rod coiled work basket with coiling spaced apart. This type was used for storage or gathering of seeds or pine nuts. Devil's claw was used in the simple decoration.*

Size: 13" diameter x 7½" deep.

R.M.M.

Panamint

(A)

(B)

(C)

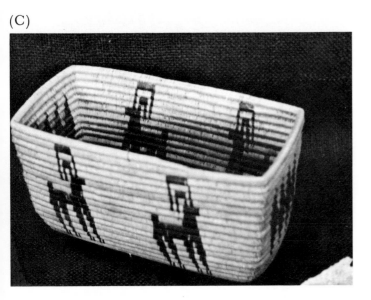

(D)

(A) *Hat worn chiefly by women but men were known to use a hat when carrying loads employing the tumpline across the forehead. The design is of devil's claw.*

Size: 8½" diameter x 5½" deep.

B.M.M.

(B) *Beaded trinket basket. The basket is coiled of willow and the beads are on thread and sewn to the basket. It is possible this beaded work is an adaptation from the Pomo feathered basket. This is a very attractive basket.*

Size: 2¾" deep x 4½" diameter.

B.M.M.

(C) *A twined grasshopper basket used to dip grasshopper in boiling water. This is not a very attractive basket and few are to be seen in collections.*

Size: 5" lip x 10" diameter x 16" deep.

R.M.M.

(D) *Deep tray coiled basket used for storage or gathering. This is a good design, well decorated, using devil's claw to form the double triangles or what has been called a butterfly pattern.*

Size: 10" diameter x 6" deep.

R.M.M.

Northern Paiute

(A)

(B)

(C)

(D)

Northern Paiute (Continued)

(E) A seed gathering fan for whipping grass seeds into a gathering basket.

Size: 10" x 19" width x 1¼" deep.

R.M.M.

(F) Winnowing or gathering tray closely twined with black dyed strips in warp and weft.

Size: 14½" x 8½" width.

B.M.M.

(G) Conical burden basket for carrying bulky loads. This basket is twined of willow with some strands dyed for pattern. The carrying loops are hemp or twine.

Size: 24" wide x 20" deep.

R.M.M.

(H) Trinket basket made by a spaced coiling technique leaving sections of the single rod coil exposed. The dark portions are devil's claw.

Size: 3½" diameter x 2" deep.

Northern Paiute

(E)

(F)

(G)

(H)

SOUTH WEST

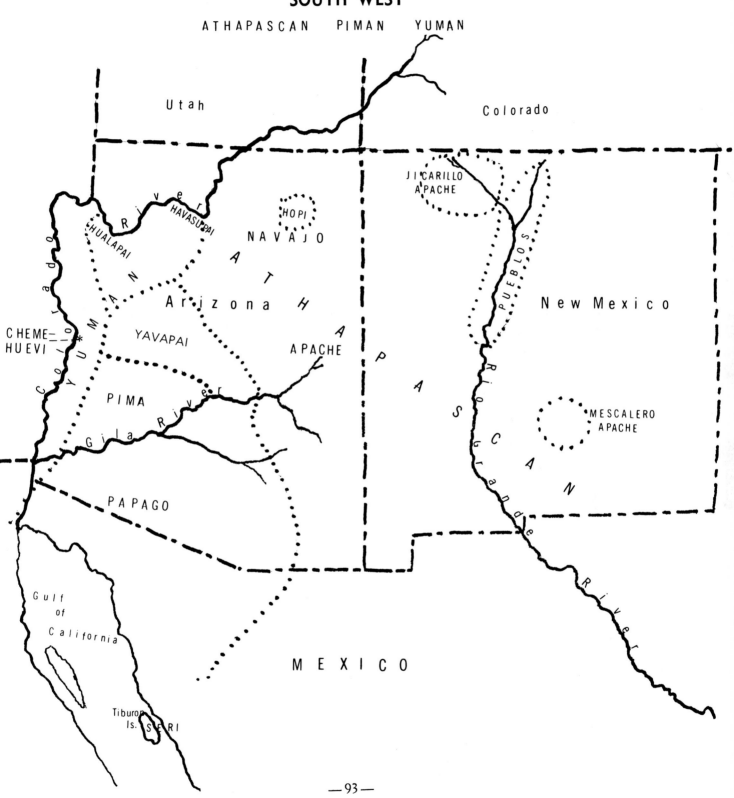

ATHAPASCAN   PIMAN   YUMAN

Utah

Colorado

Colorado River

HAVASUPAI

HUALAPAI

HOPI

NAVAJO

JICARILLO APACHE

ATHAPASCAN

Arizona

PUEBLOS

New Mexico

CHEME-HUEVI

YAVAPAI

APACHE

YUMAN

PIMA

Gila River

Rio Grande

MESCALERO APACHE

PAPAGO

Gulf
of
California

MEXICO

Tiburon
Is.   SERI

Rio Grande River

Southwest Basket Makers

The mere mention of the southwest will bring to many readers a picture of Indians making and selling their baskets, rugs, pottery and silver work. This is not too surprising for the Indians of this area have had long association with the white man and learned early of his desire to buy their crafts.

For thousands of years, Indians have known and lived in this great land area. The first were wandering hunters who lived by following game herds, but as conditions changed over the centuries they developed a more sedentary society and were among the first of the American Indians to develop a form of agriculture. When first observed by white men they were well advanced in the growing of maize, squash and beans. This dependence on agriculture demanded they establish homes of a sort in order to care for their crops.

Basketry became very important for harvesting, carrying and storing crops. The women weavers were not content to provide simple utility forms. Most used their weaving to express themselves in beautiful forms and designs woven into the baskets.

It is in the ancient southwest burial caves that we find the evidence of the "Basket Maker I" period. One human infant burial with a carbonized twined basket has been dated at 3,786 B.C. by radiocarbon assay.

The development of pottery and the introduction of the horse and sheep by the early Spanish changed the culture greatly, but the weaving of baskets held its place through all this change and until quite recent times was of great importance to the Indians in their daily lives as well as in their ceremonials.

The coming of the railroad through the heart of Indian country and the great number of travelers created an increased interest in Indian crafts, which could be purchased at every station stop.

Basket forms changed somewhat at this period. The Indians learned quickly to make the shapes and designs which would sell. Many small souvenir baskets exist today and are not the best of the Indian art work. The serious collector soon learns to be selective as there are beautiful old baskets to be found and cherished.

The basket makers of the southwest come from three major language groups, the Yuman, the Athabascan, and the Piman. In addition, the Hopi were linguistically Shoshonean and the Pueblo group in New Mexico were from Keresan, Tanoan and Zunian stocks. The basket culture crossed very few language boundaries. In fact, the reverse is true, people of the same language made different baskets, as among the Pima and Papago. The material at hand was probably the greatest influence on basket making.

Chemehuevi

This branch of the Shoshonean family and their basketry is a favorite of this writer. Their coiled basketry excelled and few others have ever developed the ability to produce zoomorphic forms as they did. Whether they depicted bird, butterfly, lizard or snake, it became a thing of beauty when woven into a basket design. They also did other designs as a star form and beautifully balanced geometricals.

They used willow and Martynia (devil's claw) for the weft or sewing material. They were acquainted with juncus and used it for a light brown color in their baskets. The red shaft of the flicker may be found in small areas of some of the older baskets.

The Chemehuevis originally split away from the Shoshoni and moved south and west along the Colorado River, but disagreement with the Mojaves drove them to the California desert country and some of their basketry techniques seem to be influenced by the southern California Mission and Cahuilla weavers, including the right hand or clockwise coiling as opposed to the general counterclockwise coiling of most Arizona Indians.

Most of the remaining Chemehuevis are now living on the Colorado River Reservation south of Parker, Arizona. The Colorado River Indian Tribes Museum on the reservation now possesses and displays the finest of their baskets.

(A) *Storage jar (Olla) coiled with willow over willow bundle. The black design is of devil's claw (Martynia). Note the black coil at lip of jar. This is the usual finish for these weavers.*

Size: 12" diameter x 8" deep.

C.R.I.T.

(B) *Large coiled tray with beautiful patterns. The butterfly is done with devil's claw and the dark portion of juncus. The Chemehuevi were masters of symmetry of design and form.*

Size: 17" diameter x 2" deep.

C.R.I.T.

(C) *Coiled jar. A very popular form among the Chemehuevi. The bird forms are well executed using both devil's claw and juncus for design.*

Size: 7½" diameter x 6½" deep.

C.R.I.T.

(D) *Coiled tray using a beetle design. This is another example of the use of zoomorphic forms. The tightness and fineness of the weave is notable.*

Size: 15" diameter x 1¾" deep.

C.R.I.T.

Chemehuevi

(A)

(B)

(C)

(D)

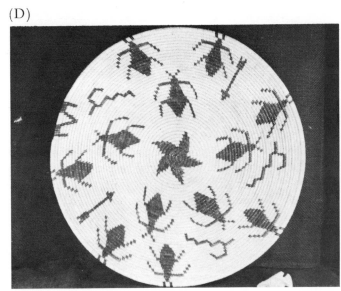

Hualapai-Havasupai

The Hualapai and Havasupai had their origin from the Yuman linguistic family which included all of lower California and extended north into California and Arizona along the Colorado River. The Hualapai wandered further north and east along the Colorado River and their culture changed. They became hunters and seed gatherers, rather than agriculturists.

The Havasupai split away from the Hualapai and, being a smaller group, sought safety from enemies by retreating to the depths of the Colorado River Canyon where they are today one of the most isolated Indian Tribes in the United States.

The Hualapai made a twined basket by what is generally called diagonal twining. The warp starting from a twist or tie at the center of the bottom extending outward and upward on a diagonal, as opposed to a vertical course to the rim which is usually finished in one or two coils. These baskets are firm and rugged. The warp is often of unpeeled twigs leaving an undertone of brown. The designs are simple bands or geometrics.

The burden basket, a deep semi-globular shape, and the pitch-covered water bottle were the common forms. The Havasupai did do some coiled trays in addition to the usual twining. These are not too common. They are quite similar in style and size to the coiled baskets of the Apache. It may not be possible to separate them without personal contact with the weaver. Obviously in the case of the older baskets this is impossible. One key may be used, the Havasupai and Hualapai rarely used animal forms on their coiled trays.

(A) *A fine coiled tray of willow or cottonwood with devil's claw for design. These trays are similar to the Apache coiled work but do not usually have animal forms.*

Size: 16" diameter x 2½" deep.

R.M.M.

(B) *The use of heavy twining strands make this basket somewhat rough in appearance. The warp is of unpeeled stems giving the entire basket a brownish color. The dark band around the basket is of devil's claw.*

Size: 8" diameter x 5½" deep.

F.L.C.

(C) *Pitch covered water jar. Horsehair loops are woven into the basket for attaching carrying straps.*

Size: 6¼" diameter x 8" deep.

R.M.M.

(D) *The Conical burden basket usually has little design. It is quite strong and will carry heavy loads. Two splints of wood are coiled around the top for rigidity and strength.*

Size: 14" diameter x 10" deep.

R.M.M.

Hualapai-Havasupai

(A)

(B)

(C)

(D)

Pima

Nearly all of the southern part of what is now Arizona was at one time occupied by the Piman linguistic group. This group includes the Papago and as a combined group they extended deep into old Mexico, as well as up into central Arizona. They were an agricultural people, dependent on the fruits of the desert and their planted crops. The Pima were not a warlike people, instead they provided food for many of the early whites who crossed their lands.

The baskets of the pima are made from willow and Martynia (devil's claw), sewn over coils of split cattail reed. Old baskets were sometimes made using cottonwood splints as the bundle. Virtually all of the Pima basketry is coiled. In earlier times a twilling technique, employing agave or cane, was used to make mats or trays. These are rarely seen now.

Some of the greatest art work seen in basketry is exhibited in the very fine old trays of the Pima. They did some traditional patterns such as the squash blossom and tortoise shell which have no equal anywhere. They also did basket jars, or ollas, which were beautifully formed and artfully decorated. The Pima favored a start of devil's claw. This made a basket with a black center. The Papago baskets usually start in white. Many of the Pima baskets finish the border with a diagonal stitch of devil's claw.

(A) *Six petal squash blossom tray made with willow over reed bundle. The black design is in devil's claw. Note black center and laced black border.*

Size: 13" diameter x 2" deep.

E.C.C.

(B) *A star and diamond design on an old basket with close coiling and symmetrical design.*

Size: 12" wide x 1" deep.

F.L.C.

(C) *Coiled tray with a traditional four petal squash blossom. These were earlier a utility form but their beauty has long since made them an item of trade.*

Size: 12½" diameter x 2½" deep.

J.C.C.

(D) *Turtle-back tray, a traditional pattern among the Pima. This is beautifully coiled with willow and devil's claw.*

Size: 10" diameter x 2" deep.

J.C.C.

(A)

(B)

(C)

(D)

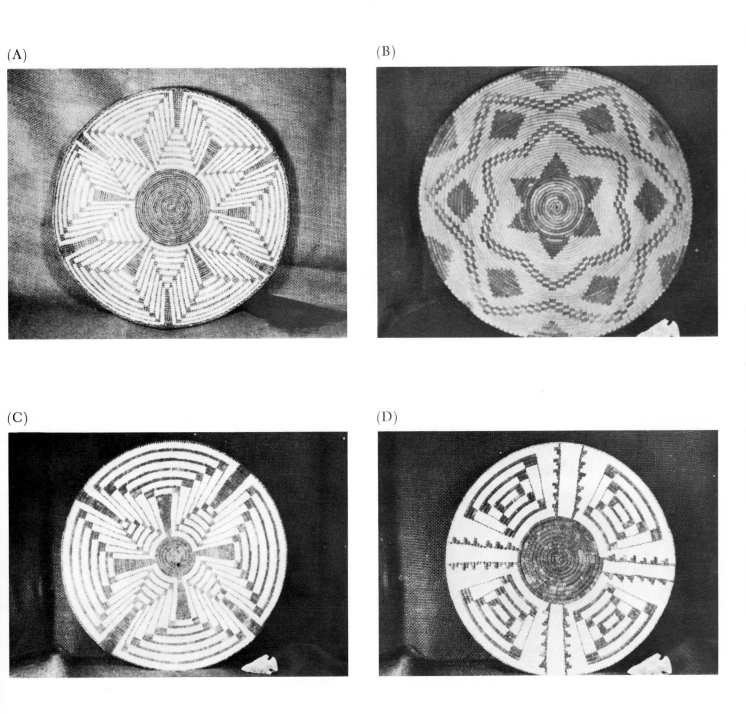

Pima (Continued)

(E) *Coiled basket with white trade beads caught on weft outlining the pattern of devil's claw (beads not sewn on). Not a usual technique of the Pima but quite attractive.*

Size: 7" diameter x 4¾" deep.

F.L.C.

(F) *A four petal squash blossom design—a very symmetrical pattern. Note the laced finish to tray border using black devil's claw.*

Size: 10" diameter x 2½" deep.

E.C.C.

(G) *Old Pima storage jar worn revealing bundles of reeds. The coiling is not tight, but the container has lasted through years of service.*

Size: 10" diameter x 12" deep.

F.L.C.

(H) *A Pima work basket with a fret design in black devil's claw with laced border. This is a utility form showing considerable use.*

Size: 10" diameter x 5" deep.

F.L.C.

Pima

(E)

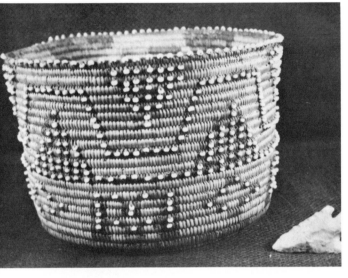

(F)

(G)

(H)

Papago

The Papago living to the south of the Pima in Arizona and along the Mexican border were prolific basket makers. At the present time they probably make more baskets than any other Indians.

Living as they do in a more arid desert environment, they use different materials than their sisters, the Pimas. Their coiled baskets utilize bear grass as the bundle, and split yucca and devil's claw for the sewing weft. These weavers do not seem bound to make any particular shape or size basket. They vary from the large grain storage olla to the miniature made of horsehair.

They make bowls, trays, and animal forms. The coil is generally larger than the coil of the Pima and gives the basket a coarser appearance. The start, or center, is not usually black and the border, or finish, is plain coiled work with no devil's claw. These are general rules and there are exceptions.

A form of basket making known as split stitch coiling has become very popular with the Papago and many baskets of this form are now for sale. They do not compare with the good old baskets but some are very well done and are quite collectible.

(A) *A trinket basket coiled on beargrass bundle. The shaded area on each side of the black devil's claw step design is done by use of the green yucca leaf.*

Size: 6" diameter x 3½" deep.

F.L.C.

(B) *The basket owl has been popular among these weavers for many years. It may have had traditional significance but is now a popular trade item.*

Size: 4½" diameter x 8" to 11" depth.

E.C.C.

(C) *A modern basket made by using a split stitch of yucca fiber over a bundle of beargrass. The grass is darker and the over-all effect is quite pleasing in such a symmetrical basket. The lid is closely fitted.*

Size: 7" diameter x 6" deep.

F.L.C.

(D) *The coiled basket with lid is a common form for the Papago. The lids are nearly always well fitted and make a nice trinket basket.*

Size: 6" diameter x 8½" over-all.

R.M.M.

Papago

(A)

(B)

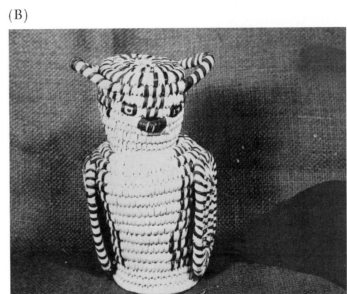

(C)

(D)

Western Apache

(San Carlos Apache, White Mountain Apache, Yavapai)

The Apache were a fearless and at times a warlike tribe, though a great deal of their conflict was an attempt to protect their homelands. From their contact with the Spanish they acquired horses and became familiar with firearms, making them equal to or superior to our frontier armies until overwhelmed by the pressure of numbers. Their homeland covered a great part of eastern Arizona and western New Mexico, extending into old Mexico. They did make raids on their neighbors, the Pima, seeking food from these agriculturists at harvest time.

The baskets of the Western Apache are generally coiled using willow and devil's claw over rods of willow or cottonwood. These baskets were in the form of trays or jars (ollas). The latter often decorated with man, horse, and dog forms. The trays, many of them of large diameter, were decorated using various star forms, employing devil's claw as the sewing weft to make the designs.

The Apache burden basket is outstanding. It is reinforced and decorated with buckskin on the bottom and as long fringes around the basket. These baskets were carried with the aid of a tumpline over the forehead of the carrier. They were made by twining over vertical rods and finished at the top rim with a coil over a heavy rod making a rugged basket.

The Apaches made a water olla or jug using this same twining technique incorporating strong wooden elbows into the basket as a place to fasten carrying lines of rope or buckskin. The olla was completely waterproofed using the pitch of pine trees.

The Yavapai are included in the Western Apache group because their basketry is indistinguishable from that of the Apache. The Yavapai are truly of Yuman stock but were held prisoner at San Carlos with the Apaches for so long that the resulting basketry culture is identical.

(A) *The large olla or jar form was used among the Apache for storage. Figures of man, woman, dog and horse were favorite designs. Devil's claw (Martynia) was used as the black element over willow or cottonwood making a strong and beautiful basket.*

Size: 20" diameter x 24½" deep.

R.M.M.

(B) *A tray with a strikingly different pattern worked to a very pleasing effect. Note the black center or start and the black finish at rim. Both are usual with Apache weavers.*

Size: 16½" wide x 4" deep.

R.M.M.

(C) *Large trays were common among the Apache. This tray with human figures undoubtedly told some story which is lost in antiquity. This basket was collected before 1900.*

Size: 21" wide x 4" deep.

R.M.M.

(D) *This basket might have been started as the base for a larger basket. Note the sets of feet around the border. A buyer offering a good price probably interrupted the weaving.*

Size: 13¾" wide x 3½" deep.

R.M.M.

Western Apache

(A)

(B)

(C)

(D)

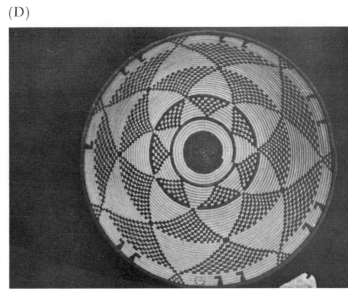

Western Apache (Continued)

(E) *The Apache burden basket is a strong well designed basket twined with heavy withes over a standing warp and reinforced with a strong twig coiled at the rim. Nearly all burden baskets were reinforced and decorated with buckskin. The bottom was covered with skin to prolong the wear.*

Size: 13" wide x 15" deep.

T.P.C.

(F) *Small jar probably made for sale. The small size would not be used for storage of grains or food. These weavers liked to have a balanced design.*

Size: 4" base x 7" x 8" deep.

B.M.M.

(G) *The water jug of the Apache seldom has a pointed bottom. It has elbows of wood woven into the basket to make a point of attachment for a carrying strap. The jug is heavily saturated with pitch to waterproof.*

Size: 5" x 12" diameter x 14" deep.

R.M.M.

(H) *The use of heavy dark patterns was common among these weavers, often making the light elements stand out as the finer design. The star pattern is popular.*

Size: 18½" wide x 3" deep.

B.M.M.

Western Apache

(E)

(F)

(G)

(H)

Mescalero Apache

This Apache group roamed over a great expanse of the southland before the encroachment of the Spanish and early American frontier settler. The Rio Grande was a lifeline for them and at one time they followed it deep into the Texas Big Bend area. It was impossible for them to long escape confinement and eventually they ended on their present small reservation area in south central New Mexico. They were given the name of Mescalero by the Spanish because of their use of Mescal, a type of cactus, as food.

The baskets of these Indians are distinctive. They use a coil of three rods, held side by side to make a flat coil and sew this coiling with split yucca leaves and yucca root bark. Their designs are bold, usually a star form or a pyramid. The use of variable green and white yucca leaf and the brown root bark makes a pleasing finish. These baskets are usually tray forms. However, ollas are to be seen.

The mescalero make virtually no baskets today. If you have the good fortune to possess one, protect it well.

Jicarilla Apache

This comparatively small tribe, belonging to the Athapascan language family is the only Indian tribe bearing the name "basket." Jicarilla, the name given them by the Spanish, means literally cup or small basket. Apparently at the time of contact with the Spanish this tribe made many small baskets.

The Jicarilla Apache were at one time intermediary between plains Indians and pueblo cultures. They were finally settled in northwest New Mexico and no longer roam the plains.

The basket forms seen may be tray, jar (olla) or deep storage types. These baskets are rather roughly made but are quite strong. They usually show some design in black and a dark red done with dyes coloring the weft materials which are withes of willow or cottonwood. The coil is usually rods of the same materials. The Jicarilla may be making some coiled baskets. There has been an attempt to revive interest in their weaving.

MESCALERO

(A) *A storage jar (olla). Note the flat appearance of the coils, due to the placing of three rods side by side before sewing with yucca leaf.*

Size: *14" diameter x 16" deep.*

T.P.C.

(B) *The tray is a more common form. The yucca leaf sewing material varies from white to green. The bark of the root is a dark brown used for design finish.*

Size: *21" wide x 3½" deep.*

R.M.M.

JICARILLA

(C) *A small basket jar, a true "Jicarilla." It was probably a personal trinket storage basket. It has heavy coiling with some of the weft dyed a dull red.*

Size: *5½" wide x 4½" deep.*

R.M.M.

(D) *A deep storage or carrying basket employing heavy rods in the bundle and coarse coiling weft. This same weft material (willow or cottonwood) is dyed red and green to make the design.*

Size: *18" wide x 24" deep.*

B.M.M.

Mescalero Apache

(A)

(B)

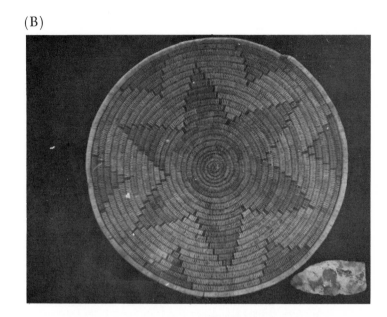

Jicarilla Apache

(C)

(D)

Navajo

The Navajo belonged to the same language group as the Apache but their culture was quite different. They were more inclined to agriculture and after contact with the Spanish and acquiring sheep a great deal of the efforts were diverted to tending their flocks. The shearing, carding, spinning, and weaving of the wool almost completely replaced the basket making of these people. Trading of woolen blankets for baskets was for them a sound business procedure. Ceremonial baskets are still used by the Navajo and it is probable that most of these baskets have been or are made by their neighbors to the north; namely, the southern Paiutes or southern Utes. It is possible that some baskets may still be made by the Navajos themselves.

A characteristic of the Navajo ceremonial tray is the herringbone edge or finish of the basket. The usual pattern or design encircles the tray except for an opening or pathway to the outside of the circle. The finish of the basket is always opposite this opening in the design. It was reported before 1900 that this tray was used as a drum. The drum stick was made of yucca leaves wrapped and sewn together. The opening in the pattern, the start of the coil, and the finish at the border must be in line. This line should point east and west when the tray is being used in any ceremony.

(A) *Coiled ceremonial tray. The center band is dark red dyed weft. The triangle pointing out and in from this band are black of devil's claw.*
Makers of (A) and (B) unknown.

Size: 13" diameter x 3" deep.

B.M.M.

(B) *Coiled ceremonial tray. The major design is nearly always the same. Small variations will be noted—all have the herringbone border.*

Size: 16½" diameter x 3" deep.

R.M.M.

(C) *A modern basket known to be made by the southern Utes. The same pattern as (A) and (B) are used as well as the same colors. The edge is finished in herringbone weave.*

Size: 13" diameter x 3½" deep.

R.M.M.

(D) *Detail of the edge weave used in all Navajo Ceremonial baskets. The finish point of this weave is always opposite the open line in the pattern of the tray.*

(A)

(B)

(C)

(D)

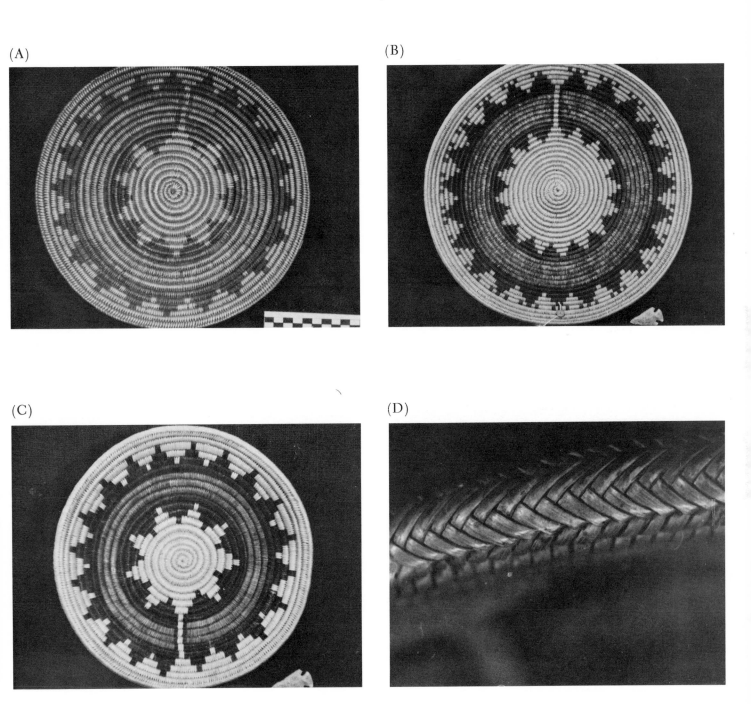

Hopi

This family of Shoshonean speaking people have during all of historic time existed in separation from others of the same language. They settled on three main mesas in what is now northern Arizona. They were and are completely surrounded by the Navajos. Theirs is a pueblo culture with permanent homes on the mesa and agricultural crops in spring-fed areas at the base of the mesas.

The arts and crafts of the Hopi vary from one mesa to another. The basketry of the Second Mesa is nearly always done in coiling, sewing the coils with yucca fiber over bundles of grass forming shallow trays. Occasional deep coiled baskets are made. Use of dyed fibers for creating a design is common. Usual colors are red, yellow, and black.

The Third Mesa weavers rarely make coiled baskets. Instead they use a technique recognized as wickerwork. They, too, do mostly plaques or shallow trays with occasional deep baskets also done in wicker. They dye the rabbit brush material to colorful greens, reds, yellows and black.

The Hopi still make baskets as well as excelling in other crafts as pottery and silverwork. The First Mesa Hopi do mostly pottery and few baskets.

(A) *Coiled bowl of yucca. The coiling bundle is of shredded yucca stems and the sewing weft is yucca leaf. The yucca is dyed colors of yellow, orange, red, green and black to produce colorful design.*

Size: 5" wide x 4½" deep.

E.C.C.

(B) *Old coiled plaque of yucca in colors of yellow, green and red, but not as brilliant as the modern dyes.*

Size: 11" plaque.

B.M.M.

(C) *Twilled work basket of split yucca leaves. This type has been made by both Second and Third Mesa weavers. It is a strong but undecorated basket.*

Size: 14" diameter x 2" deep.

(D) *Detail of the yucca leaf sewing on yucca stem shreds completely covering the bundle.*

Hopi
(SECOND MESA)

(A)

(B)

(C)

(D)

Hopi (Continued)

(A) *Deep wicker basket. Rabbit brush weft is woven in and out over framework of wild currant. This deep basket form developed as a sale item. Yucca leaf is used to coil the finished border.*

Size: 6" base x 13" lip x 12" deep.

B.M.M.

(B) *Detail of the wicker weave and the yucca coiled border. Note no twining is used.*

(C) *Highly decorated and colored wicker plaque of rabbit brush with yucca leaf border dyed black. Leaf border dyed black. The colors of the plaque are yellow, orange, red, blue and black.*

Size: 11½" plaque.

E.C.C.

(D) *Sifting tray of rabbit brush. This is a utility form used to remove sand from corn kernels.*

Size: 16" diameter x 2" deep.

F.L.C.

Hopi
(THIRD MESA)

(A)

(B)

(C)

(D)

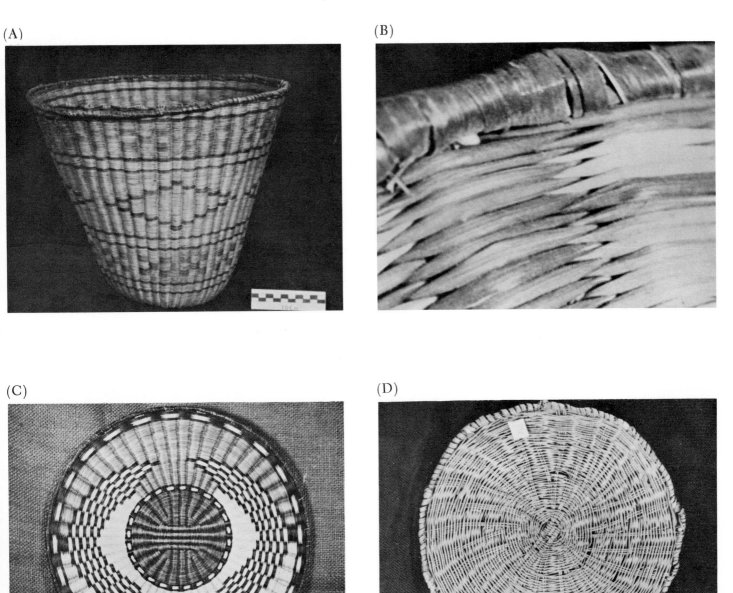

Pueblo

The Pueblos of the Rio Grande valley in upper New Mexico were never really famous for their basketry but in many old collections are found a type of wickerwork which is not seen in other Indian work. Six or seven withes of willow are worked together making a firm and quite attractive basket. This technique may have been introduced by early white teachers or traders but I find no record of this and I like to believe that the Indians were the true originators.

The baskets illustrated are from museum collections and are attributed to Tesuque and Santo Domingo. There is little or no distinction between them. These were collected sixty to eighty years ago. The Pueblos make no baskets today.

(A) *Wicker basket from Pueblo of Santo Domingo showing weaving of six strands together.*

Size: 17" wide x 4½" deep.

R.M.M.

(B) *A smaller wicker basket utilizing six strands as a warp and single strands on the lower one-half as the weft.*

From the Pueblo of Tesuque.

Size: 6" diameter x 2" deep.

A.S.M.

Pueblo

(A)

(B)

Seri

Only some fifty years after Columbus discovered America, the Seri Indians were discovered on their small island homeland by the Coronado expedition. Even though they had this early contact with civilization, they have managed to remain isolated and hold on to their primitive culture better than most any other existing Indians. They are nomadic within their domain depending on natural supplies of food from the land and seas. Basketry is an old art among them.

Using a coiling technique, not too different from that of the Papago, they make a very solid and usable basket. Two forms are usually made, an olla and a shallow tray. Both are utilitarian, being used for storage and food handling about the camp. They use fibers of the Torote as both coil and sewing material. The torote fibers are sometimes dyed a dark brown to make simple geometric designs.

(A) *Seri storage basket from fibers of torote, a fibrous desert plant. The diamond design is common.*

Size: 15" diameter to 5"

13" deep

B.M.M.

(B) *Seri tray in a utility form. It is tightly coiled with torote root and the design is done by dying the torote a brown color. This color is achieved by boiling the torote with the root of a plant called "koesayway."*

Size: 15" diameter x 4" deep.

F.L.C.

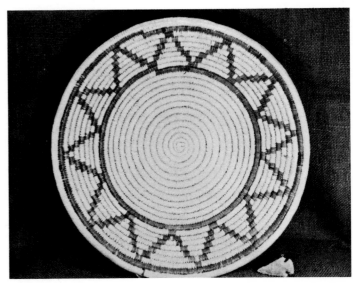

SOUTH EAST

Iroquoian

No Carolina

C H E R O K E E

Tenn.

So. Carolina

M U S K H O G E A N

*
CHOCTAW

*
KOASATI

Mississippi

Alabama

Georgia

Florida

asat

*
CHITIMACHA

S E M I N O L E

CHITIMACHAN   MUSKHOGEAN   CHEROKEE (IROQUOIAN)

rk.

Southeastern Basket Makers

As history moves, it was only a short step from the landing of Christopher Columbus in the western world to the settlement of the Spanish on the mainland of southeastern North America along the coasts of what is now North and South Carolina, Georgia and Florida. It was not a long step until the Gulf shores were to be settled by both Spanish and French. A long while before the coming of the white man the Indians had inhabited much of these coasts and a great part of the inland areas. Their legends have it that their ancestors came from the west, crossing a great river and finding good homes among the headwaters of the many creeks which flowed south and eastward. They were thus named "the Creeks" by early explorers. These people were of the Muskogean linguistic family and would later comprise the Choctaw, Chicasaw, Alabama, Koasati, Seminole and others. That these people were early basketmakers is attested by history, but few examples of really ancient work were preserved. Some descendants of the Creeks—the Koasti, Alabamas, Choctaws, and the Seminoles still make a few baskets. Cane splints, pine needles, and grass coils are the materials used. The modern coiled work now commonly employs raffia and thread as the sewing materials. The cane baskets are twilled and some are very well made.

In southern Louisiana, west of the Mississippi River, near its delta, were two lesser tribes of Indians, the Attakapan and the Chitimacha. These tribes did fine baskets employing cane splints. The Chitimacha did probably the finest cane basket in the world. To handle one, observing its beauty of color, form and construction, is a great thrill for an admirer of baskets. These latter tribes have virtually disappeared today and no more weaving is being done. Due to the durability of the cane work, many pieces have survived and, if recognized, can be saved from destruction.

The Cherokee, belonging to an entirely different linquistic family, will be considered among the southeastern tribes. This great weaving group are of Iroquoian stock. They may have been the parent stock of the Iroquois who for all of historic time have occupied the area around Lake Erie, Lake Ontario and the St. Lawrence River.

The Cherokee did, and still do, make fine baskets, even though they have been divided and scattered from North Carolina to Oklahoma. Tourists and collectors have kept a market alive for good weavers among them, especially those who reside in western North Carolina. Hopefully, a desire for quality baskets will keep this art form alive.

Chitimacha

This comparatively small tribe, living on the Mississippi River Delta of Louisiana, was responsible for some of the most beautiful work to be done anywhere using native cane. Their very name, given them by the Choctaws, literally means, "they possess cooking vessels."

The baskets they made are not only pleasing in form, but employe various colors: buff, black, brown, red and yellow to create beautiful geometrics. Many of their more intricate baskets are double woven, a basket within a basket, requiring great skill and dexterity. Many of their baskets are supplied with a very well fitted lid. All of their work is twilled. Cane lends itself to this technique very well, allowing for beautiful patterning.

It is commonly believed that the cane weaving of the southeast Indians may have originated with the Chitimacha and radiated north and east to the Choctaw, Creek tribes and the Cherokee. The techniques are even related to some South American Indian work. A Chitimachan basket is to be treasured.

Koasati

(Coushatta)

The Koasati, a Muskhogean language group, originally belonging to the Creek confederacy, broke away and moved westward from Alabama about 1800 and finally settled in Louisiana near the small town of Elton. They have great pride in the fact that their lineage is nearly pure. They own their lands and are self-supporting.

They still make some baskets, mostly for sale to the occasional visitors to their settlement. The weavers have adapted form and colors to be marketable. They make a twilled cane basket and have developed a technique of coiling the needles of the native pines into a very pleasing basket. The sewing material used is raffia, utilizing a split stitch and leaving the coil open to make the baskets more attractive.

CHITAMACHA

(A) A *wallet or cigar case of fine cane twilling in colors of yellow, orange and black. These are double woven—a basket within a basket. The finest cane work to be seen.*

Size: *5" depth x 3" width.*

R.M.M.

(B) *Utility cane basket twilled in colors of yellow, orange, brown and black in a symmetrical pattern.*

Size: *6¾" square x 2" deep.*

R.M.M.

KOASATI
(Coushatta)

(C) *A nicely formed pine needle basket with coils of long needles of pine sewn with a heavy fiber grass using split stitch. Designs laid on using dyed grasses.* (Recent)

Size: *12" diameter x 6" deep.*

F.L.C.

(D) *A recent twilled cane basket. This is a brave attempt to copy the old type basketwork, a nearly lost technique.*

Size: *8" wide x 9" length x 2" deep.*

F.L.C.

Chitimacha

(A)

(B)

(C)

(D)

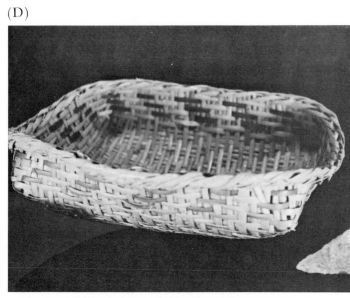

Choctaw

The Choctaw employed cane almost exclusively for their baskets. Their baskets were not so finely made nor as colorful as the Chitimachas but were quite well made and attractive. A favorite form among the weavers was an oval top and a pointed bottom representing a heart shape equipped with a handle. These baskets were called gift baskets and indicated that the gift was from the heart.

(A) *A good example of an old Choctaw twilled cane gift basket. This double opening basket used as a carrying purse is in colors of natural cane and black.*

B.M.M.

(B) *Heart-shaped cane twilled gift basket. (Carrying the gift from the heart of the giver.)*

Size: 3" wide to 11" wide.

12" overall height.

R.M.M.

(C) *Heart-shaped cane basket without a handle. It is done in very fine twilling in tri-colors of natural, brown and black.*

Size: 5½" wide (upper part) x 4" deep.

R.M.M.

Choctaw

(A)

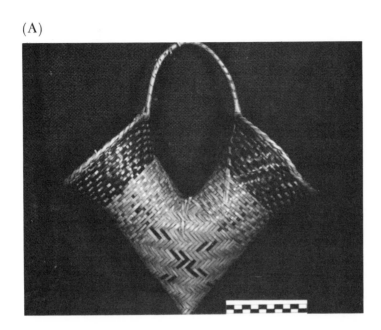

(B)

(C)

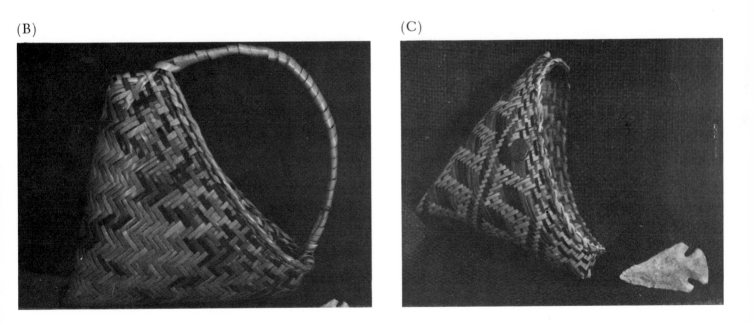

Seminole

The Seminole are chiefly a Muskhogean linguistic group of Indians who broke away from the Creek confederacy in the early 1700's.

The name Seminole was given this group by the Muskogee Indians and means literally "wild" or "wild ones." They moved southward from Georgia and eventually settled in what is now Florida. The history of their being driven into the swampy Everglades is a bloody and unsavory one.

The Seminole had their origin as a tribe in historic time and had early contact with traders. Aboriginal arts were unimportant for existence; however, basket making continued. Today they make a grass coiled basket using cotton thread of various colors as the sewing material. The basket commonly has a palmetto bottom and often a decorated top bearing a head with hairdress and beads. The overall result is usually pleasing and is worth collecting. No cane baskets are made by the Seminole.

(A) *Recent Seminole basket of grass coils sewn with blue and red thread. The bottom is a circle of palmetto. The lid has a head done in palmetto and beads. The headdress is not a hat but depicts an old style dressing of the hair.*

Size: 8" diameter x 3½" deep.

6½" overall.

F.L.C.

(B) *Coiled basket of grass bundles sewn with reed strips. This is not a common technique.*

Size: 7" diameter x 3" deep.

(C) *Coiled on grass bundles and sewn with weft of colored thread. The loop handles are a simple extension of the body coil. The basket has a closely fitted lid.*

Size: 7" diameter x 2" deep.

F.E.C.

(D) *A plain straight side basket coiled on grass bundle. It is sewn with grass as a weft and was probably a personal trinket basket.*

Size: 4½" diameter x 2" deep.

Seminole

(A)

(B)

(C)

(D)

Cherokee

The Cherokee who shared a boundary with the Creek tribes on the south were an entirely different linguistic group. They were Iroquoians. There is still some differing of opinions as to origin of the Iriquois tribes, but if we follow the basket cultures it appears that this group originated in the southeast and migrated northward into the area of Lake Erie, Lake Ontario and the St. Lawrence River.

Very early reports as that of Mr. James Adair writing "History of the American Indians," London, 1775, mentions the excellent clothes baskets made by the Cherokee using cane strips. The baskets were one and one-half foot wide and three feet long, eight or ten made to nest with each other. Cane baskets are not commonly made any more but are still collectible.

The Cherokee cane is not as finely made as the Chitimacha with simpler designs and is almost always finished at the border with an oak hoop bound on with hickory bark fiber. Most recent baskets are made of oak, ash, or maple splints.

Many ethnologists believe the twilled weaving of cane originated in southern Louisiana and the art then spread north and east until it reached the Cherokee. Since cane was not plentiful in the mountainous country in which they lived, it is not difficult to see how they changed to a different material as the oak splint.

The use of the splint apparently spread northward to be adapted by many of the northeastern Algonquin Indian groups infringing on the early use of birch-bark containers.

The Cherokee continued to make some baskets even after great numbers of them were forcibly moved to Oklahoma. Some nice baskets are still sold to tourists in western North Carolina where a few Cherokee attempt to hold on to some of their native culture.

(A) *Hickory with ash splint, made in North Carolina. This is a variation of the melon basket. This form is modern and probably developed only for sale.*

Size: 9" long x 3½" wide x 11" high.

E.C.C.

(B) *Cane twilled basket in three colors—natural cane, brown and black. An old basket similar in technique to the Chitimacha of Louisiana. Note the hickory splint coiled to the top. This is characteristic of Cherokee.*

Size: 10" diameter x 12" deep.

E.C.C.

(C) *A strong hickory splint basket from the Oklahoma Cherokee, a real work basket. Note coiled splint on top. There is no decoration on this basket.*

E.C.C.

(D) *Honeysuckle basket in wickerwork with a fitted lid. The basket is well made and is attractive. Note the hickory splint around the edge of the lid.*

Size: 8" diameter x 4½" deep.

E.C.C.

Cherokee

(A)

(B)

(C)

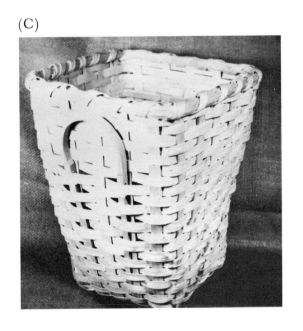

(D)

Cherokee (Continued)

(E) *Carrying basket with hickory splint handle. It is highly decorated in dyed cane in colors of brown and black. A hickery splint is coiled to lip of basket for strength.*

Size: 13" wide x 8½" deep.

(F) *Hickory and ash splint basket with hinged lids. This ribbed type with depressed center of bottom is sometimes called a melon basket because of its shape.*

Size: 7" wide x 8" long x 4" deep.

R.M.M.

Cherokee

(E)

(F)

NORTHEAST

ALGONQUIAN   IROQUOIAN

ESKIMAUAN

Baffin Is.

E S K I M A U A N

Hudson

Bay

Quebec

A L G O N Q U I A N

ntario O

Ojibwa

St. Lawrence River

Micmac

Chippewan

L.Superior

Nova Scotia

Penobscot

L.Huron

L. Ont.

L.Michigan

Mohawk

L.Erie

I R O Q U O I A N

United States

Northeastern Basket Makers

All of the northeast is the homeland of the Algonquin speaking people with the exception of the inclusion of the Iroquoian tribes around Lake Erie, Lake Ontario, and along the St. Lawrence River.

The great Algonquin tribes occupied the greatest expanse of land of any American Indian group. They reached from Hudson Bay to southern Illinois and from British Columbia in Canada to Newfoundland, Nova Scotia, and southward as far as Maryland. They were chiefly woodland dwellers and at an early time used chiefly birch bark containers called Makuks. It has been mentioned when discussing the Cherokee that it is possible that the Iroquoian group may have

introduced basket making to the Algonquin. They do follow a similar technique. The use of the wood splint is common throughout the northeast. Some of the Algonquin tribes to the west still do chiefly birch bark containers, many heavily decorated with porcupine quills.

The baskets of the northeast also include the use of sweet grass in several ways. It is sometimes braided and included in the weave. At other times, sweet grass is used as decorative roll bound to be finish edge of a basket and often as a decorative handle. This grass adds, not only to the beauty of the basket, but is a pleasure to the sense of smell. It retains its sweet pleasant fragrance for years.

Algonquians

The discussion of this widespread linguistic family under one heading would seem to be impossible, but many of them did not make baskets and their basketmakers were limited in type. The early types of containers were actually not baskets at all but were made of sheets of birch bark sewn together and sealed with pitch to be waterproof. This was called a "Makuk."

It is theorized that the Algonquian tribes began to weave a basket only after their contact with the Iroquoian families. The western tribes of Algonquian who have had little contact with the east and the Iroquois still make chiefly the birch bark type of container, usually highly decorated with porcupine quills. The woven baskets of the Micmac, Malicseet and the Penobscot bear a strong similarity to the baskets of the Iroquois and Cherokee (Iroquoian family). The Chippewa and Ojibwa used both the birch bark and wicker weaving. The material for weaving among the Chippewa was chiefly willow branches, the peeled branch making the lighter color and the unpeeled blighted branches used to get a brown or red color stripe. They commonly made what is known as a mellon-shaped basket, a very strong and practical work basket for gathering or storage. A very nice basket was acquired from Mrs. Margaret Aas of Warroad, Minnesota, in 1970. Hopefully she has taught others to weave as well.

Sweet grass is used for weaving decorative and trinket baskets among most of the tribes where it is available. It is a good and strong weaving material and its pleasant aroma adds to the pleasure of having the basket.

The Ojibwa make many small trinket baskets of birch bark, usually decorated with porcupine quill, dyed in many colors, and often finished at the border with a roll of sweet grass.

(A) *Closeup detail of weave using ash splints with a variation called porcupine weave because of the projections of the loop.*

(B) *Micmac*
A porcupine basket with lid. This loop weave was often used and makes an attractive basket. The lid uses ash splints in combination with braided sweetgrass and a roll of sweetgrass around the rim.

Size: 7½" diameter x 3" deep.

(C) *Penobscot*
A recent (1968) basket by Josephine Francis of Old Town, Maine, using ash splints and braided sweetgrass. The colored bands are yellow, green and brown dyed by leaching water from crepe paper.

Size: 9" diameter x 12" deep.

F.L.C.

(D) *Micmac*
A well formed melon basket of wood splints. This is a strong utility basket, beautiful in shape and finish, with dyed strips of brown for decoration.

Size: 10½" diameter x 5" deep.

F.L.C.

Algonquian

(A)

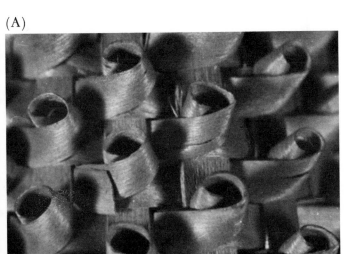

(B)

(C)

(D)

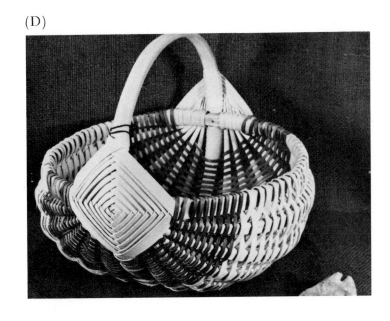

Algonquian (Continued)

(E) *Old Chippewa birch bark with porcupine quill design in white, yellow and red coiled sweetgrass border sewn with black thread.*

Size: 10½" diameter.

B.M.M.

(F) *Ojibwa*
Birchbark completely covered with porcupine quillwork with a beaver design in red-brown dyed quills. Sweetgrass borders are on lid and base of basket.

Size: 4½" diameter x 2" deep.

F.L.C.

(G) *Recent (1970) Chippewa basket by Margaret Aas of Warroad, Minnesota. It is a willow wickerwork design of unpeeled withes making a strong work basket.*

Base: 13½" diameter x 9½" deep.

F.L.C.

(H) *Ojibwa*
Old "Makuk" of birchbark. It is a water-tight container and might have been a berry picking basket. The lip is reinforced with willow sewn in and rawhide loops added.

F.L.C.

Algonquian

(E)

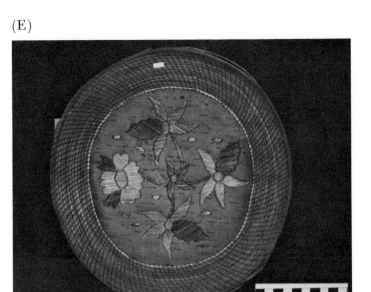

(F)

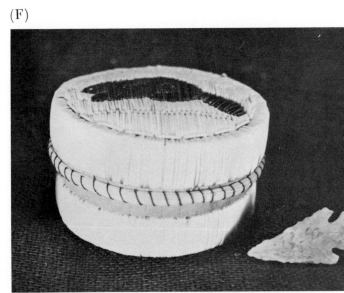

(G)

(H)

Iroquois

It was not too many years after Columbus landed in the West Indies that the French were exploring in the area of the St. Lawrence River. In 1535, Cartier reported on wars among the Indians of this area. The Algonquin were probably the chief opponents, although it is known that the warlike Iroquois had considerable unrest among themselves. Much has been recorded of the conflicts of the past, but little true information has come down about the arts and crafts at this early period of contact.

Early illustrators did show some type of burden basket in use, but details are lacking. If we accept the theory of northward migration of the Iroquoian family from the south, then we assume the basketry forms followed the early cane weaving of the lower Mississippi River tribes. The use of cane would be replaced by other wood materials. This seems most logical for the basket types recorded and collected later were of this wood splint type, using checkerweave or wickerwork. The pounding of green wood of ash to separate it into its sap layers was an early technique for making mats and baskets. The withes of willow were a natural material for the wicker type weavings.

The Iroquois tribes were separated widely after the revolutionary War due to the allegiance of the greater part of these people with the British. Many moved north of the St. Lawrence River and the Great Lakes of Erie and Ontario. It is in this area that today the Mohawks still make some nice baskets. In northern New York state some baskets have been made until recently in a feeble attmpt to keep alive some of the early arts and crafts.

(A) *Ash splint basket with a variation of the checkerweave. The lacelike border is made by looping narrow splints.*

Size: 6" diameter x 2¾" deep.

R.M.M.

(B) *A recent (1967) basket by the Mohawks near Brantsford, Ontario, using dyed wood splints and braided sweetgrass for a very pleasing basket.*

Size: 10" diameter x 4" deep.

F.L.C.

(C) *Splint basket from upper New York (1910-15). Sweetgrass, a commercial cord, and dyed wood splint are incorporated around the top and bottom.*

Size: 6" diameter x 4" deep.

F.L.C.

(D) *Old basket from Brantsford, Ontario, in the form of a purse with handle, one side fitting closely into other side. Some braided sweetgrass is used in body and at the borders.*

Size: 9¾" diameter x 4½" deep.

F.L.C.

Iroquoian
(MOHAWK)

(A)

(B)

(C)

(D)

Eskimo

(Eskimauan)

These dwellers of the far north have developed hand-crafts in many forms, using ivory, stone, bone, skin, furs and the native grasses. They are capable of doing fine artistic work in all of the above materials.

Basketry was probably introduced to them by adjacent Indians or Europeans. They are no longer noted for the finest weaving. Other crafts have superseded the slow processes of basket making. A pair of sealskin moccasins can be made with less effort and time than a basket and will bring a better return in the market.

Baskets are still made by some using the wild rye or lyme grass which grows in the far north. Some willow is used when available. The type of basket and the technique vary generally according to location and seems to depend greatly on their teachers. Thus, on the west coast of Alaska the baskets tend to follow the techniques of the Aleuts, however never quite reaching the same plane of excellence. Many modern baskets have lid handles carved from ivory or stone. The technique of weaving is generally coiling. Some start over a solid skin bottom, avoiding the difficult start of a coiled basket. The so-called ginger jar is a popular shape, as well as a straight sided bandbox with a lid The Eskimo artist is capable of excellence but tends to become careless if people will pay for poor work. This is not an exclusive Eskimo trait.

The Eskimo far to the east and around Hudson Bay did make a very fine coiled basket unlike anything done by the Algonquin who are their neighbors to the south. I cannot trace any introductory origin except European, unless the culture lines extend all the way to the Bering Sea, which is not an impossibility. These eastern Eskimo used more decoration, nearly always introducing a dark pattern of triangles or squares in the weft. They also like to leave triangular openings in

(A) *Coiled grass mat. It could have been made for trade. The open triangular coiling is well shown here. The design is dyed red and brown grass weft.*

Size: 10" diameter.

B.M.M.

(B) *Very closely coiled ginger jar type with dyed grass weft design in simple blocks. The lid is well fitted.*

Size: 4½" diameter x 6" deep.

F.E.C.

(C) *Coiled grass bowl with flat lid which is not usual. Triangle design in pale colors of red and black of dyed weft.*

Size: 6¾" diameter x 5" deep.

R.M.M.

(D) *Old jar coiled with variation in center, circumferential coil to make handle. The design in weft by use of animal skin, possibly from skins of sea birds.*

Size: 5" diameter x 5½" deep.

R.M.M.

Eskimo
(EASTERN)

(A)

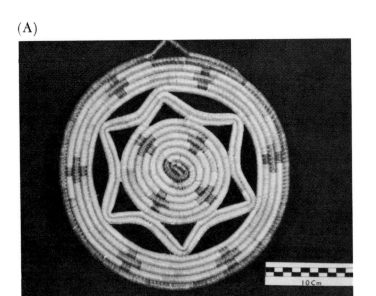

(B)

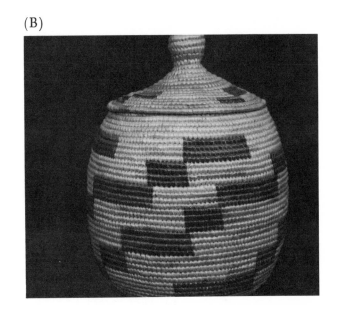

(C)

(D)

Eskimo (Continued)

the coiled weave, usually two or more rows completely around the circumference of the basket. A very well fitted lid with a knob at its top was a finishing touch for such a basket.

Occasionally an Eskimo basket will be decorated with a few trade beads. Even the claws of aquatic birds have been so used.

(A) *A popular ginger jar shaped, coiled basket of lyme grass with trade beads sewn to animal skin then onto basket for decoration.*

Size: 4½" diameter x 5½" deep.

A.S.M.

(B) *Personal storage basket of coiled grass, decorated with dark (dyed) animal skin or sinew. The lid tie is of undyed skin.*

Size: 10½" long x 4½" wide x 3½" deep.

A.S.M.

(C) *Recent basket (1965) from Great Whale River of coiled lyme grass with carved stone lid handle.*

Size: 5½" diameter x 3" deep.

F.L.C.

(D) *Woven grass inner socks made by twining. The same technique used on old mats.*

Size: 10½" long foot.

B.M.M.

Eskimo
(WESTERN)

(A)

(B)

(C)

(D)

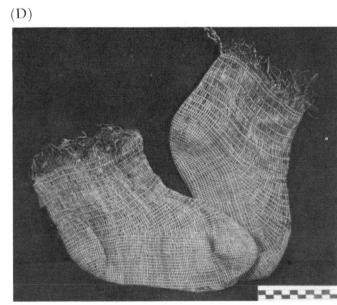

Alphabetical List of Basket Making Tribes
of North America

This list is revised from Otis T. Mason's *Aboriginal Indian Basketry—Report of National Museum* 1902

Abenaki, Algonquian Family, Maine and Canada.

Aleut, Aleutian Islands.

Algonquian Family, Northern frontier and Canada, many tribes.

Apache, Athapascan Family, several tribes from Arizona, New Mexico.

Ashochimi, Yukian Family, near Healdsburg, California.

Atsuge, Hat Creek, branch of Pit River.

Attakapa, Attakapan Family, southern Louisiana.

Attu. (See Aleut.)

Bella Coola, Bilhula, Salishian Family, northwestern British Columbia.

Cahuilla (Coahuilla), Shoshonean Family
  Cahuilla, Kawia, Agua Caliente, Santa Rosa, Cabezon, Torres, Twenty-nine Palms and Saboba, southern California.

Cayuse, Waiilatpuan Family, Umatilla, Oregon.

Chehalis, Salishan Family, Washington.

Chemehuevi, Shoshonean Family, Arizona and California boundary.

Cherokee, Iroquoian Family, North Carolina and Oklahoma.

Chitimachas, Chetimachan Family, Louisiana.

Chickasaw, Muskhogean Family, southeast, U.S.

Chilcotin, Athapascan Family, British Columbia.

Chinook, Chinookian Family, lower Columbia River, Washington.

Chippewa, Algonquian Family, northern United States.

Choctaw, Muskhogean Family, Louisiana.

Chukchansi, Yokut Tribe, north of Fresno, California.

Chumash, Moquelumuan Family, southwestern California.

Clallam, Salishan Family, Washington.

Coconinos (Havasupai), Yuman Family, Arizona.

Cowlitz, Salishan Family, Washington.

Creeks, Muskhogean Family, southeastern United States.

Dieguenos, Yuman Family, San Diego County, California.
  Capitan Grande, Sequan, Santa Isabel, Cuyamaca and Morongo.

Diggers, Pujunan Family, vegetable eaters, east of Sacramento, California.

Eskimo, Eskimauan Family along Arctic Sea.

Fraser River, Salishan Family, British Columbia.

Haida, Skittagetan Family, southern Alaska, Queen Charlottee Islands and British Columbia.

Hat Creek, Palainihan, northeast California.

Havasupai, Yuman Family, Arizona.

Hoh, Chimakuan Family, (Quilleute), Neah Bay, Washington.

Hopi (Moki), Shoshonean Family, northeastern Arizona.

Hualapai (Walapai), Yuman Family, northwestern Arizona.

Hupa (Hoopa), Athapascan Family, northwestern California.

Iroquois, Iroquoian Family, northeast Great Lakes and St. Lawrence River.

Jicarilla Apache, Athapascan Family, northern New Mexico.

Karok, Quoratean Family, Lower Klamath River, California.

Kaweah, Mariposan Family, middle California.

Klamath, Lutuamian Family, Klamath County, Oregon.

Klikitat, Shahaptian Family, Washington and Oregon.

Koasati (Coushatta), Muskhogean Family, Louisiana.

Lillooet, Salishan Family, western British Columbia.

Luiseno, Shoshonean Family, San Luis Rey, California.

Lummi, Salishan Family, north Puget Sound, Washington.

McCloud, Copehan Family, northern California.

Maidu, Pujunan Family, east of Sacramento River from Sacramento, California, to Honey Lake.

Alphabetical List (Continued)

Makah, Wakashan Family, Cape Flattery, Washington.

Malicseet, Algonquian Family, Nova Scotia.

Maricopa, Yuman Family, southern Arizona.

Melicite (Malicseet), Algonquian Family, Quebec and New Brunswick.

Menomini, Algonquian Family, northeastern Wisconsin.

Mescalero Apache, Athapascan Family, New Mexico.

Micmac, Algonquian Family, Nova Scotia and Quebec.

Missions, many different villages, Shoshonean and Yuman Families, southern California.

Miwok, Moquelumnan Family, north central California, east of San Joaquin River to Sierras.

Modoc, Lutuamian Family, east of Mount Shasta to Goose Lake, California and Oregon.

Mohawk, Iroquoian Family, Ontario, Canada and New York.

Mojave, Yuman Family, lower Colorado River.

Monos, Shoshonean Family, east of Yosemite to desert, California.

Navajo, Athapascan Family, northern Arizona.

Nehalem, Salishan Family, Oregon.

Nez Perce, Shahaptin Family, northeastern Oregon and Idaho.

Nisqualli, Salishan Family, Columbia River, Washington.

Nutka (Nootka), Wakasha Family, West Vancouver Island.

Ojibwa, Algonquian Family, Michigan and Canada.

Paiutes, Shoshonean Family, California and Nevada.

Panamint, Shoshonean Family, Death Valley, California.

Papago, Piman Family, southern Arizona.

Penobscot, Algonquian Family, Old Town, Maine.

Pima, Piman Family, Arizona.

Pit River, Palaihnihan Family, Pit River, California.

Pomo, many divisions, Kulanapan Family, Mendocino and Lake Counties, California.

Pueblos of Rio Grande, Tanoan and Keresan Families, (Tesuque) (Santo Domingo), New Mexico.

Puyallup, Salishan Family, Puget Sound, Washington.

Quilleute, Chimakuan Family, northeastern Washington.

Quinault, Sahishan Family, West Washington.

Salishan Family, varied techniques and many tribes, Washington and British Columbia.

San Carlos Apache, Athapascan Family, southeastern Arizona.

Santa Barbara (Chumash), Moquelumnan Family, southwestern California.

Seminole, Muskhogean Family, Florida.

Seri, Yuman Family, Tiburon Island, Sonora, Mexico.

Shasta, Sastean Family, Shasta and Scott Valley, California.

Shoshoni, Shoshonean Family, Great Basin area, Montana.

Shushwap, Salishan Family, British Columbia.

Siletz, Athapascan Family, Oregon.

Skagit, Salishan Family, North Puget Sound.

Skokomish, Salishan Family, Puget Sound.

Snohomish, Salishan Family, Puget Sound.

Spokan, Salishan Family, east Washington and Montana.

Tahoe, Washoan Family, Lake Tahoe, California.

Tejon, Tulares of Tejon Pass, Moquelumnan Family, California.

Thompson River, Salishan Family, British Columbia.

Tinne, Athapascan Family, Alaska and Canada.

Tlinkit, Koluschan Family, southeastern Alaska.

Tolowa, Athapascan Family, northwestern California.

Tulares, Moquelumnan Family, central California.

Ute, Shoshonean Family, Utah.

Wasco, Chinnokan Family, Columbia River, Oregon.

Washo, Washoan Family, western Nevada and eastern California. (Lake Tahoe)

White Mountain Apache, Fort Apache, eastern Arizona.

Wikchumni, Yokut tribe, Mariposan Family, Sierra Region, California.

Wiyot, small Algonquian Family Group, northwestern California.

Wintun, Pit River Indians, Copehan Family, northern California.

Yavapai, Yuman Family, Arizona.

Yoalmani, Yokut Tribe, Mariposan Family, Tule River, California.

Yoerkali, Yokut Tribe, Mariposan Family, Tule River, California.

Yokuts, several groups, Mariposan Family, middle California.

Yurok, Algonquian Family, Klamath River, California.

Bibliography

Amsden, Charles, *The Ancient Basketmakers*, Southwest Museum Leaflet No. 11, Southwest Museum, Highland Park, Los Angeles, California.

Ariss, Robert, *Indians of Western North America*, Los Angeles County Museum, 1955.

Bahti, Tome, *Southwestern Indian Arts and Crafts*, KC Publications, Flagstaff, Arizona, 1964.

Bahti, Tom. *Southwestern Indian Tribes*, Ibid, 1968.

Balls, Edward K., *Early Uses of California Plants*, University of California Press, Berkeley, 1965.

Barrett, S. A., *The Washo Indians*, Bulletin of the Public Museum of the City of Milwaukee, Vol. II, No. 1, May 1917.

Barrett, S. A., *The Material Culture of the Klamath and Modoc Indians of Northeastern California and Southern Oregon*, American Archaeology and Ethnology, Vol. V, No. 4, June 1910, University of California.

Barrett, S. A., and Gifford, E. W., *Miwok Material Culture*, Cannon Printing Co., Milwaukee, Wisconsin, 1933.

Barrows, David Prescott, *The Ethno-Botany of the Coahuilla Indians of Southern California*, Malki Museum Press, Morongo Reservation, Banning, California, 1967.

Boas, Franz, *Ethnology of the Kwakiutl*, Thirty-fifth Annual Report of the Bureau of American Ethnology, Part I—1913-1914, Govt. Printing Office, 1921.

Boas, Frank; Haeberlin, H.K.; Teit, James A.; and Roberts, Helen H., *Coiled Basketry in British Columbia and Surround-Region*, Forty-first Annual Report of the Bureau of American Ethnology 1919-1924, U.S. Government Printing Office, Washington, D.C., 1928.

Brandon, William; edited by Alvin M. Josephy, Jr., *The American Heritage Book of Indians*, American Heritage Publishing Co. Inc., 1961.

Breazeale, J. F., *The Pima and His Basket*, Arizona Archaeological and Historical Society, 1923, Acme Printing Company, Tucson, Arizona.

British Columbia Heritage Series, Introduction to Our Native Peoples, Series I—Vol. 1, 1951, Provincial Archives, Provincial Museum, Victoria, B.C.

Coast Salish, Series I, Vol. 2, Ibid, 1952.
Interior Salish, Series I, Vol. 3, Ibid, 1952.
Haida, Series I, Vol. 4, Ibid, 1952.
Nootka, Series I, Vol. 5, Ibid, 1952.
Tsimshiam, Series I, Vol. 6, Ibid, 1952.
Kwakiutl, Series, I, Vol. 7, Ibid, 1953.
Kootenay, Series I, Vol. 8, Ibid, 1952.
Dene (Athapasca), Series I, Vol. 9, Ibid, 1953.
Queen Charlotte Islands, Series II, Vol. 1, Ibid, 1953.

Cain, H. Thomas, *Pima Indian Basketry*, Heard Museum of Anthropology and Primitive Art, McGrew Printing and Lithographing Co., 1962.

Cressman, L. S. *The Sandal and the Cave*, Beaver Books, Portland, Oregon, 1964.

Curtain, L. S. M., *Some Plants Used by the Yuki Indians of Round Valley, Northern California*, (Historical Review and photographs by Margaret C. Irwin), Southwest Museum Leaflets, Number 27, 1957, Highland Park, Los Angeles, California.

Dawson, Lawrence; and Deetz, James, *A Corpus of Chumash Basketry*, Archaeological Survey, Annual Report, University of California Press, 1965, pp. 197-276.

Densmore, Frances, *Chippewa Customs*, Bureau of American Ethnology, Bulletin No. 86, U.S. Government Printing Office, Washington, D.C., 1929.

Densmore, Frances, *Uses of Plants by the Chippewa Indians*, 44th Annual Report of the Bureau of American Ethnology, U.S. Government Printing Office, Washington, D.C., 1928.

Emmons, G. T., *Memoirs of the American Museum of Natural History*, 1903, Vol. II, The Basketry of the Tlingit.
Vol. III, Anthropology.

Haeberlin, H. K.; Tiet, James A.; and Roberts, Helen H., *Coiled Basketry in British Columbia and Surrounding Region*, 41st Annual Report of the Bureau of American Ethnology, 1919-1924, U.S. Government Printing Office, Washington, D.C., 1928.

Harrington, John P., *Exploration of the Burton Mound at Santa Barbara, California*, 44th Annual Report of the Bureau of American Ethnology, U.S. Government Printing Office, Washington, D.C., 1928.

Harrington, John P., *A New Original Version of Boscana's Historical Account of the San Juan Capistrano Indians of Southern California*, Smithsonian Miscellaneous Collections, Vol. 92, No. 4, June 27, 1934.

Heizer, Robert F., *One of the Oldest Known California Indian Baskets*, "The Masterkey," April-June, 1968, Southwest Museum, Highland Park, Los Angeles, California.

Hewes, Gordon and Hewes, Nina, *Indian Life and Customs at Mission San Luis Rey*, (translation of "A Record of California Mission Life," written by Pablo Tac, 1835), Old Mission San Luis Rey, California, 1958.

Hodges, Frederick W., *Handbook of American Indians North of Mexico*, Pageant Books, Inc., New York, N.Y.

James, George Wharton, *Indian Basketry*, Private Printing, Pasadena, California, 1902.

Johnston, Bernice Eastman, *California's Gabrielino Indians*, Southwest Museum, Los Angeles, California, 1962.

Kibby, Leo P., *California, The Civil War, and The Indian Problem*, Journal of the West, Vol. IV, No. 3, July 1965, p. 377-410.

Kirk, Ruth E., *Panamint Basketry*, "The Masterkey," Vol. XXVI, No. 3, May-June, 1953.

Kroeber, A. L., *Handbook of the Indians of California*, Bureau of American Ethnology, Bulletin 78, U.S. Government Printing Office, Washington, D.C., 1925.

Bibliography (Continued)

Kroeber, A. L., *Basket Designs of the Mission Indians of California*, American Museum of Natural History, Vol. XX, Part II, 1922.

Lyford, Carrie A.,*Ojibwa Crafts*, Phoenix Indian School, 1943.

Lyford, Carrie A., *Iroquois Crafts*, Haskell Institute, 1945.

Mason, Otis Tufton, *Aboriginal Indian Basketry*: Studies in a Textile Art Without Machinery, Report of the U.S. National Museum under direction of the Smithsonian Institution for year ending June 30, 1902.

Mason, Otis Tufton, *The Human Beast of Burden*, pp. 237-295, Annual Report, Smithsonian Institution, 1887, Part II.

Mason, Otis Tufton, *Cradles of American Aborigines*, p. 161-212, Annual Report, Smithsonian Institution, 1887, Part II.

Mason, Otis Tufton, *Basketwork of North American Aborigines*, pp. 291-307, Annual Report, Smithsonian Institution, 1884, Part II.

Merriam, C. Hart, *Studies of California Indians*, University of California Press, Berkeley and Los Angeles, California, 1955.

Miles, Charles, *Indian and Eskimo Artifacts of North America*, Bonanza Books, 1963.

Miller, Ronald Dean and Miller, Peggy Jeanne, *The Chemehuevi Indians of Southern California*, Malki Museum Press, Banning, California, 1967.

Moriarty, James Robert, *Evidence of Mat Weaving from an Early La Jolla Site*, "The Masterkey," Vol. 40, No. 2, April-June 1966, Southwest Museum, Highland Park, Los Angeles, California.

Mosley, N. Edward, *The Discovery and Definition of Basket Maker—1890 to 1914*, "The Masterkey," October-December 1966, Southwest Museum, Highland Park, California.

Neill, Wilfred T., *Florida Seminole Indians*, Great Outdoors Association, St. Petersburg, Florida.

Orcutt, Ada M., *Tillamook. Land of Many Waters*, Tillamook County Pioneer Museum Commission, Metropolitan Press, Portland, Oregon, 1951.

Pepper, George H., *The Ancient Basket Makers of Southeastern Utah*, Supplement to American Museum Journal, Vol. II, No. 4, April 1902, Guide Leaflet No. 6.

Point, Nicholas, S. J. (Translation by Joseph P. Donnelly) *Wilderness Kingdom*, Loyola University Press, Chicago, Illinois, 1967.

Powell, J. W., *Eighteenth Annual Report of the Bureau of American Ethnology* to the Secretary of the Smithsonian Institution, 1896-97, Part I, Government Printing Office, Washington, D.C., 1899.

Purdy, Carl, *Pomo Indian Baskets and Their Makers*, C. M. Davis Company Press, 1902.

Richards, Irmagarde, *Early California*, California State Department of Education, Sacramento, California, 1950.

Riddle, Francis A. *Ethnography of Two Maidu Groups*, "The Masterkey," April-June 1968, Southwest Museum, Highland Park, California.

Roberts, Jr., Frank H. H., *Late Basketmaker Site in the Chaco Canyon, New Mexico*, Bureau of Ethnology, Bulletin 92, Government Printing Office, Washington, D.C., 1929.

Robinson, Bert, *The Basket Weavers of Arizona*, University of New Mexico Press, Albuquerque, New Mexico, 1954.

Sauer, Carl, *The Distribution of Aboriginal Tribes and Languages in Northwestern Mexico*, Ibeno-Americano: 5, University of California Press, 1934.

Speck, Frank G., *Decorative Art and Basketry of the Cherokee*, Bulletin of the Public Museum of the City of Milwaukee, Vol. 2, No. 2, Milwaukee, Wisconsin, 1920.

Steward, Julian H., *Ancient Caves of the Great Salt Lake Region*, Bureau of American Ethnology, Bulletin 116, 1937, U.S. Government Printing Office, Washington, D.C.

Stewart, Kenneth M., *The Kiva*, Journal of the Arizona Archaeology Historical Society, Vol. 34, No. 1, October 1968.

Stewart, Kenneth M., *Mojave Indian Agriculture*, "The Master Key," January-March 1966, Southwest Museum, Highland Park, California.

Stirling, Mathew W., *Indians of the Americas*, National Geographic Society.

Swanton, John R., *Early History of the Creek Indians and Their Neighbors*, Smithsonian Institution, Bureau of American Ethnology Bulletin 73, U.S. Government Printing Office, Washington, D.C., 1922.

Swanton, John R., *Social and Religious Beliefs and Usages of the Chicasaw Indians*, 44th Annual Report of the Bureau of American Ethnology., U.S. Government Printing Office, Washington, D.C., 1928.

Swanton, John R., *Aboriginal Culture of the Southeast*, 42nd Annual Report of the Bureau of American Ethnology, 1924-1925, U.S. Government Printing Office, Washington, D.C., 1928.

Swanton, John R., *The Indian Tribes of North America*, Bureau of American Ethnology, Bulletin 145, U.S. Government Printing Office, Washington, D.C., 1952.

Tanner, Clara Lee, *Southwest Indian Craft Arts*, University of Arizona Press, 1968.

Teit, James A., *The Salishan Tribes of the Western Plateaus*. 45th Annual Report of the Bureau of American Ethnology. 1927-1928, U.S. Government Printing Office, Washington, D.C., 1930.

Underhill, Ruth, *The Papago Indians of Arizona and Their Relatives The Pima*, Branch of Education, Bureau of Indian Affairs, Haskell Institute, Lawrence, Kansas.

Bibliography (Continued)

Underhill, Ruth, *Indians of Southern California*, Branch of Education, Bureau of Indian Affairs, U.S. Department of the Interior, Sherman Pamphlets, No. 2.

Underhill, Ruth, *The Northern Paiute Indians of California and Nevada*, Bureau of Indian Affairs, U.S. Department of the Interior, 1941.

U.S. Department of the Interior, *Report on Indians Taxed and Indians Not Taxed in the United States*, Eleventh Census 1890, U.S. Government Printing Office, Washington, D.C., 1894.

Wadsworth, Beula, *Design Motifs of the Pueblo Indians*, The Naylor Company, San Antonio, Texas, 1957.

Walker, Edwin F., *Indians of Southern California*, Southwest Museum Leaflet #10, Highland Park, California.

Watkins, Frances E., *The Navajo*, Southwest Museum Leaflet #16, Highland Park, California.

Watson, Frances E., *Potlatches and a Haida Potlatch Hat*, "The Masterkey," January 1939, Southwest Museum, Highland Park, California.

Webb, Edith Buckland, *Indian Life at the Old Mission*, Warren F. Lewis, 1951.

Wyman, Anne, *Corn Husk Bags of the Nez Perce Indians*, Southwest Museum Leaflet #1, Highland Park, California.

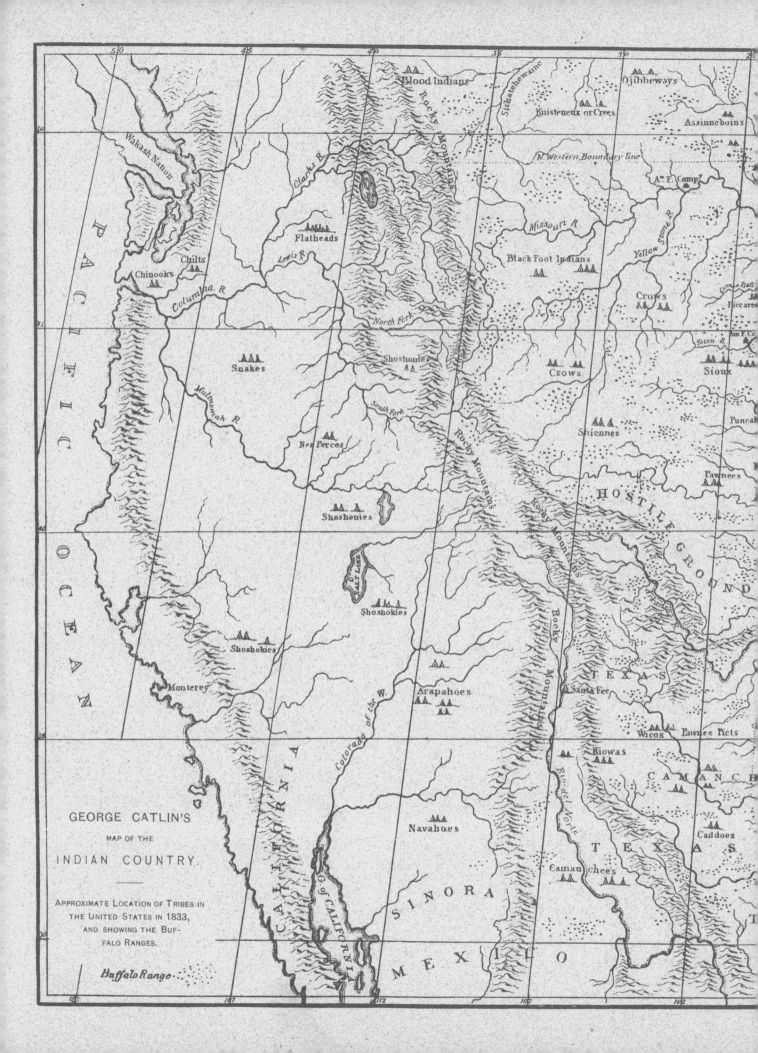

GEORGE CATLIN'S

MAP OF THE

INDIAN COUNTRY.

———

APPROXIMATE LOCATION OF TRIBES IN
THE UNITED STATES IN 1833,
AND SHOWING THE BUF-
FALO RANGES.

Buffalo Range

Blood Indians
Ojibbeways
Siskatchewaune
Knisteneux or Crees
Assinneboins
N. Western Boundary line
A. F. Camp
Wakash Nation
Clarks R.
Flatheads
Lewis R.
Missouri R.
Black Foot Indians
Yellow Stone R.
Chilts
Chinooks
Columbia R.
Crows
Canon Ball
Riccaree
Am. F. Co.
North Fork
Snakes
Shoshonies
Teton R.
Crows
Sioux
Mulhomah R.
South Fork
Nez Percos
Shiennes
Puncah
Rocky Mountains
Shoshonies
Pawnees
HOSTILE GROUND
SALT LAKE
Shoshokies
Shoshokies
Rocky Mountains
TEXAS
Monterey
Arapahoes
Santa Fee
Colorado of the W.
Wicos
Pawnee Picts
Kiowas
Rio del Norte
CALIFORNIA
Navahoes
CAMANCH
Caddoes
G. of CALIFORNIA
SINORA
Camanchees
TEXAS
MEXICO
PACIFIC OCEAN